C·A·T·C·H

T·H·E·M

THINKING

R960

A Handbook of Classroom Strategies

James Bellanca & Robin Fogarty

Permissions

Grateful acknowledgment is made to the following authors
and agents for their permission to reprint copyrighted materials:

"The Dinner Party," by Mona Gardner, © 1942 *Saturday Review Magazine.*
Reprinted with permission.

SCAMPER brainstorming technique, *SCAMPER: Games For Imagination Development*
by Robert F. Eberle, © 1971. Printed with permission of DOK Publishers, East Aurora,
New York.

Catch Them Thinking: A Handbook of Classroom Strategies
Published by **Skylight Publishing, Inc.,** 200 E. Wood Street, Suite 274, Palatine, IL 60067
Toll Free 800-348-4474 (in northern Illinois 708-991-6300) FAX 708-991-6420

© 1986 IRI/Skylight Publishing, Inc.

Graphics by Jim Arthur

Eighth Printing, July 1992

ISBN 0-932935-02-8

ACKNOWLEDGEMENTS

We would like to express appreciation to four special educators for their support on this project:

Dr. Arthur Costa of Sacramento State University in California, who promoted the concept of metacognitive processing as an implicit part of teaching for intelligent behavior.

Dr. Barry Beyer of George Mason University, Virginia, who has promoted the idea of teaching the explicit thinking skills.

Drs. Roger and David Johnson, University of Minnesota, who mentored our thinking about cooperative learning and structured interaction.

Dr. Ronald Brandt, executive editor, ASCD, who has pioneered the resurgence of interest in teaching for, of and about thinking.

Our sincere thanks to these four individuals for their leadership and influence in teaching for intelligent behavior.

TABLE OF CONTENTS

CATCH THEM THINKING:
A Handbook of Classroom Strategies

INTRODUCTION

"Thinking in the classroom?" asked the puzzled parent. "What ever happened to the basics? I don't want any of that fancy stuff. I just want my youngsters to read and write and do their math. If I didn't need any of this fancy thinking stuff when I went to school, why should they?"

When I hear such questions, and I hear them often from parents, school board members and educators, I must recognize their deep and legitimate concerns. I also must remember that this is not the 1930's, nor the 60's, nor even the early 80's. While the history of educational reform, with its contributions and its excesses, has contributed much to these concerns, more important considerations are rooted in what most of us recognize is happening today and what must happen tomorrow in our classrooms to assure every child a quality education.

When asked, "Why thinking" in the context of "the basics," I always ask a follow-up question to assure myself that we are using the same definition. Usually I find that the question comes more from a bias based on limited knowledge about basic education ("Adding, subtracting, vocabulary" and so on) or experience ("The way it was when I went to school.").

I cannot question the legitimacy of the concerns. As a parent with four children, I have felt the anxieties, shared the worries and tossed at night with all the questions about school, and success, and failure, and grades and peer pressures and what they are learning and not learning and what will happen? What I can call upon is a critical examination of what we know is happening in our classrooms and what must happen in the future so that our youngsters are as well prepared as we hope.

There are three areas in which I have found most people who ask the "why thinking" question lack important information: (1) What are basic skills? (2) What is being done about these skills in the classroom? and (3) What rationale justifies a shift in emphasis?

WHAT ARE BASIC SKILLS? For the most part, basic skills are described as reading, writing and arithmetic. While there is some disagreement on minor points, a large number of parents will describe reading as "telling what a story is about" or arithmetic, "remembering your number facts; " for writing, it is "using good grammar."

The majority of effective school districts regularly test how well their students are doing with "basic skills." An examination of one of the more widely used basic skills tests will demonstrate a somewhat more sophisticated picture of basic skills (see next page).

What does this illustrate? As a start, it suggests that what many believe to be the basic skills is in fact very short sighted. Today's students are being tested not only on computation, information recall and the mechanics of writing, but in addition, they are being asked to demonstrate their abilities to perform higher level thinking about important content. In fact, the majority of test items on many of the so-called basic skills tests evaluate more higher level tasks than the so-called "basic tasks."

And what do the results say? If we turn to the National Assessment of Educational Progress, we can get one important answer. Since 1969, this test has assessed hundreds of thousands of American students in a variety of subject areas. Every few years, the students are retested to determine whether they have improved or slipped.

First, the good news. In general, at least 75% of tested students have mastered fundamental reading, writing and arithmetic skills and there is a stability of progress in literal comprehension, writing mechanics and computation skills.

READING VOCABULARY

TRANSLATION
RECALL OF SYNONYM
1 2 3 4 5 6 7 8 9 10 11 12 13 14 15 16 17 18 19 20 21 22 23 24 25 26 27 28 29 30 31 32 33 34 35 36 37 38 39 40

READING COMPREHENSION

RECOGN. APPL.	TRANSLATION		INTERPRETATION			ANALYSIS
LITERAL RECALL	REWORDING	CONTEXT CLUES	MAIN IDEA	DESCRIP. WORDS	CONCLUSIONS	STRUCTURE/STYLE
17 24 38	7 10 19 36 37 42	11 13 31 44	1 14 22 25 28 35 39 41 45	4 6 34	2 5 8 9 12 15 16 18 20 29 40	3 21 23 26 27 30 32 33 43

SPELLING

RECOGNITION/APPLICATION	TRANS-LATION
RECALL OF RULE	CONTEXT CLUES
1 2 3 4 5 6 7 8 9 10 11 12 14 15 16 17 18 19 20 21 22 23 24 27 28 29	13 25 26 30

LANGUAGE MECHANICS

RECOGNITION/APPLICATION	
PUNCTUATION	CAPITALIZATION
1 2 3 4 5 6 7 8 9 10	11 12 13 14 15 16 17 18 19 20

LANGUAGE EXPRESSION

RECOGNITION/APPLICATION	TRANSLATION	INTERPRE-TATION	ANALYSIS
USAGE	DICTION	SYNTACTICAL RELATIONSHIPS	ORGANIZATION
21 22 23 24 25 26 27 28 29 30	31 32 33 34 35 36 37 38 39 40	41 42 43 44 45	46 47 48 49 50 51 52 53 54 55

MATHEMATICS COMPUTATION

APPLICATION			
ADDITION	SUBTRACTION	MULTIPLICATION	DIVISION
1 2 3 4 5 6 7 8 9 10 11 12	13 14 15 16 17 18 19 20 21 22 23 24	25 26 27 28 29 30 31 32 33 34 35 36	37 38 39 40 41 42 43 44 45 46 47 48

MATHEMATICS CONCEPTS

RECOGNITION	INTERPRETATION/ANALYSIS			
NUMBER SYSTEMS	NUMBER SYSTEMS	SETS	GEOM./MEAS.	PROBLEM SOLVING
2 3 5 6 7	1 4 8 9 10 14 17	16 18 19	20 21 22 23 24	11 12 13 15 25

MATHEMATICS APPLICATIONS

TRANSLATION/INTERPRETATION			ANALYSIS
NUMBER SYSTEMS	MEASURE-MENTS	PROBLEM SOLVING	PROBLEM SOLVING
26 27 28 29 30 32	33 35 36 37 38	31 34 39 41 43 44 47 49 50	40 42 45 46 48

Now, the bad news. When examining scores in areas which require more complex thinking skills, we see poor results. In reading, few students provided more than superficial responses when asked to explain a point of view and most appeared never to have learned how to draw inferences or think critically about what they were reading. In writing, few could elaborate on ideas or support arguments. In math, problem solving skills were almost non-existent.

If we accept the National Assessment's evidence, we must recognize two points. First, by more conventional understandings of "basic skills," our schools are effective with the vast majority of students. Second, on the basis of test results which identify "basics" in terms of more complex thinking processes, the schools are far less successful. This leaves us with a double challenge. On the one hand, we must help the parents and the public redefine "basic" so that they can more accurately understand what determines a child's success or failure in school. On the other hand, we must take concerted action to help our students improve in those higher level thinking areas where low performance is most noticeable.

The most immediate task is to ask "why." There are two reasons. First, the tests dictate it. Ideally, we can argue how tests should not dictate what we teach. The reality is that the tests, at least for the time being, dictate a student's future. Students are tracked by tests, admitted or rejected to schools and colleges by tests, even hired for jobs by tests. In our society, we place a very heavy emphasis on "How'd ya do?" Parents are concerned about test scores and a multimillion dollar business thrives on test preparation. In the next century, there seems little chance that we will throw out a system that our culture has worked so hard and carefully to perfect. As a consequence, I believe that we can justify the argument that our schools do a more acceptable job in preparing students to do their best according to the test standards set for them. Clearly this means we must better prepare students to think critically, to solve problems and make sound decisions.

To answer the second "why," the key is all around us. Today's student lives in an electronic, high tech world. The most conservative projections tell us that this is only the beginning. When my parents brought home that first 12″ black and white TV more than thirty years ago, I had no idea that I would be typing this introduction on an 8″ screen and sending it to an editor by electronic mail. What are the implications for my four year old daughter who already plays word and math games on a machine that I didn't know existed until graduate school? I cannot predict in detail what her work world will look like in twenty years, but I can project what quality of thinking she will need and what type of education will prepare her for that. If memorizing and regurgitating facts 96% of the time does not adequately prepare today's students for their job world, it certainly won't help in a time, two decades from now, when she will need even more thinking and problem solving skills.

The second major question is "how?" How do we teach students to become more skillful thinkers? Even though the evidence from the National Assessment describes the low performance of students as skillful thinkers, many teachers will argue that they are teaching students to think. I don't doubt that. I do wonder, however, if some who are riding in a Model T, who have never seen or driven in anything else, make the claim because they really don't understand the complexity and capability of today's car. Most of our teaching of thinking is like the Model T. It gets the driver from town to town, although not very quickly, comfortably or efficiently when compared to the improved models produced today.

In the last decade, the effective school's research and cognitive research has provided us with the means to update our school house Model T's. We have made giant strides in identifying ways to improve instruction so that all students can learn faster and better. Included in these improvements are the methodologies to help all students become more skillful thinkers.

SKILLFUL THINKING IN THE CLASSROOM

Just as it is necessary to build a tall building on a solid foundation, it is necessary to build skillful thinking in the classroom on two preconditions: (1) the teacher's mastery of the content and (2) the teacher's effectiveness in creating and managing positive conditions for thinking. Without a teacher who has mastered the subject, be it social studies, language arts, math or science, the students will lack a model who thinks about the content. Thinking skills do not work in a vacuum. They are not content free. They are immersed in some content. Just as the football player doesn't learn blocking skills in isolation from content, the student's mastery of thinking skills is imbedded in the content. Just as the coach, with experience and knowledge of the game, introduces the right skill at the right time for each player, the skilled teacher does the same for her thinking students.

A second important element is the teacher's skill as an effective classroom manager. The most effective thinking skills instruction won't cure a chaotic or disruptive classroom. Nor will it bring to life a classroom that is controlled only by fear. At the very least, the teacher must be conducting a classroom in which students know and follow basic rules and there is a strong, on-task atmosphere well-grounded in respect and responsibility.

Given these preconditions, the soil is ready to plant the seed for critical and creative thinking. The thinking classroom is a classroom in which the teacher purposefully gives priority to teaching students multiple ways to think about what they are learning. In a concrete sense, this means she will structure opportunities for guided practice of the thinking skills, and teach the students how to transfer these skills into more difficult content. She will shift the emphasis in the classroom from a content/product orientation to a content/thinking process approach.

We live in a time of information overload. Faster than we can grasp the information that rains down on us each day, radical new discoveries are uprooting traditionally accepted theories. One university professor lamented to his students at the close of a medical course that 50% of the information he had given in the course would be obsolete before they received their degrees. He went on to add that his biggest dilemma was the fact that he couldn't even tell them which half it would be!

We only need to look around us to see the professor's point being corroborated time and time again. In 25 years, the computer has shrunk in size from a two-story building accessible only to high level graduate students to a tiny microchip hidden in every car, thermostat and electrical appliance that is sold. Mail, not long ago trapped in week-long delivery schedules across town, now flies electronically around the world in minutes. Mass production jobs disappear from the want ads and are replaced by calls for computer programmers, technicians and high-tech engineers.

While the work, home, and leisure worlds have changed in the last two decades more rapidly than we could anticipate, only one world has remained essentially the same. Almost immune to improvement and innovation, the school seems forever trapped in the information acquisition model begun with the Gutenberg Press. The school house has done all it can to ignore the real power of the computer. Using a pre-chip mentality, schools change the curriculum solely by adding more: more information (compare a high school U.S. History text of 25 years ago with one published this year. Note how much more information is jammed into the same course which 25 years ago couldn't cover all the information); more courses (everyone who suffers from the "facts are learning" disease wants to plug another course into the curriculum: driver's education, substance abuse, parenting, and so on); more of everything...except perhaps quality.

Most serious teachers are frustrated with the "cover it" mentality which has resulted from the "more is better" mentality. "In the same amount of time, cover everything in the curriculum including what we added this year." This translates to "don't slow down if students are struggling. Don't stop for an indepth look at an important skill or concept. Don't investigate." There is not time. Just "Hurry up, hurry up or you'll be late." "Mrs. Smith's class," says the complaining parent, "is four chapters ahead." And what about the departmental exam that covers the whole book? Or the supervisor who asks: "Shouldn't you be further...?"

John Goodlad has addressed this rat race in *A Place Called School*. As his researchers saw it, few are the classrooms in which the teachers do more than pump out information to their students. They saw teachers who talk, students who listen. Teachers construct scan-tron tests, students check off the facts. Ultimately, nationally standardized tests tell us that these same students cannot problem solve, think critically or argue logically to support a position.

To prepare our young people for the possibilities and probabilities of the future that few of us can imagine, the wisest course seems to be a curriculum that triggers their critical and creative thinking. The computer will store more information better than the most brilliant learner. By causing students to think, question, wonder, explore, analyze, debate, hypothesize, create and use wisely the avalanche of information they will encounter every day, an in-depth curriculum that focuses on thinking skills will provide more fertile ground for their intellectual growth in a high tech world.

Given such a curriculum, every classroom teacher will have a major responsibility to promote every student's skills for thinking. The teaching technology exists by which any of us can change our classroom from the present pool of passivity to an action lab of active thinking.

However, rather than ask teachers to reinvent the wheel, we need only recognize, as Ron Edmonds did "that the technology exists. We need only the will." That technology, which is expanding every day, begins with the effective teaching research and includes methodologies proven to work in classrooms, not only with gifted students, but with students with learning disabilities, students with little interest in schools, high school students and kindergarten students.

Anyone who has been in school must concede that as teachers, we possess an almost absolute power within the classroom. Bruce Joyce says that "teaching is the second most private behavior." According to Marilyn Ferguson in *Aquarian Conspiracy*,

"Even doctors, in their heyday as godlike paragons, have never wielded the authority of a single classroom teacher, who can purvey prizes, failure, love, humiliation, and information to a great number of relatively powerless, vulnerable young people."

Based on this belief that the teacher is without exception the key figure in the classroom, let's consider some important implications: the impact of teacher expectations, the roles the teacher plays in a 'thinking classroom,' cognitive research and the important methodology available for promoting skillful thinking.

1. *Expectations*: Thomas Good's research on teacher expectations offers convincing evidence that when teachers *expect* high quality learning, students sense these subtly disguised expectations and tend to live up to (or down to) them.

If and when teachers believe that all students *can* think...and all students *need* to think, that message *is* communicated to the students. Teachers who value thinking challenge all students to stretch. These teachers cause students to interpret, analyze, translate, hypothesize, predict, apply, synthesize and evaluate what they learn. They expect students to discuss, debate, answer higher level questions, prove, write, think aloud and critically and creatively attack the ideas shared by the teacher, the texts and peers.

These teachers are *mindful decision-makers*, who take the time to dig deeply into carefully selected key ideas; who force thinking responses from all students; who ask probing questions and expect thoughtful answers from all students; who develop all students' thinking skills, and find new methods to challenge even the most reticent. In short, teachers' expectations for excellence in all students is modeled repeatedly in overt and deliberate teaching behaviors.

The key to high expectations, however, is more than commanding students to "think harder" and "think harder again." The telltale sign of high expectations in a classroom is the teacher's behavior toward low performing students. These are the students generally perceived as not doing their work, hiding in the back of the classroom, clowning around or regularly off task for one reason or another.

Good's research indicates that teacher perception of student behavior is a major shaper not only of overt misbehavior, but also of self-concepts, achievement motivation and levels of aspiration.

Just as Henry Higgins was able to change Eliza Doolittle's self beliefs, so too every classroom teacher has an expectation impact on students. Some students learn from repeated praise, attention and success that they are expected to do very well. They strive to live by that expectation. Others, year after year, get the signals that they are slow, awkward and poor workers. After a while they learn to act as they are expected.

Good and others have traced specific teacher behaviors which communicate to many students that not much is expected in the classroom. For one reason or another, very often through unconscious stereotypes of race, sex or class, the teacher perceives certain students to be low academic performers. As a consequence, he communicates that low performance is all anyone can expect. These low expectations are communicated in a number of subtle ways.

What else does the research show about the low performers? Teachers smile at them less often, make less eye contact, call on them less, praise them less, give them less feedback, demand less effort and criticize them more. In the meantime, the same teachers give more wait-time, more cues and more follow-up questions to the students perceived as being more active learners.

The low performers find seats farther away from the teacher. This makes it easy for them to avoid monitoring and to slip into off-task behavior. In the meantime, those who see themselves as the high performers grab the front row. (Some call this the Sunday Church Syndrome. If you don't want to be there, hide in the back pew and exit fast.)

Although it may seem that teachers who promote thinking by all students must do everything except divide the Red Sea, their challenge is considerably less. Starting with the belief that all children can learn to think more critically and creatively, the effective teacher need do little more than add to her repertoire of skills and methodologies that promote skillful thinking. For examination, these are divided into four categories: teaching FOR thinking, by setting the climate; teaching OF thinking, by presenting the explicit skill; teaching WITH thinking, by structuring the interaction; and teaching ABOUT thinking, by metacognitive processing. But first, let's look at another key factor in the thinking classroom.

2. **Teacher Roles**: What roles do teachers play that demonstrate the value they place on thinking? To promote genuine 'thinking' in the classroom, teachers take tremendous risks. As a high school physics teacher said: "In a thinking classroom, the sage must abdicate the stage." The teachers who foster thinking in the classroom make a conscious decision to give up their autonomy in that classroom. They relinquish 'center stage' and instead assume several enabling roles. They are leaders who assume various, strategically effective roles dictated by circumstances. Marilyn Ferguson described the classroom leader in this way:

> "The open teacher...establishes rapport and resonance, sensing unspoken needs, conflicts, hopes and fears. Respecting the learner's autonomy, the teacher spends more time helping to articulate the urgent questions than demanding right answers...The teacher is...a midwife to ideas...a steersman, a catalyst - a facilitator - an agent of learning..."

In addition, the works of Blanchard & Hersey (*Situational Leadership*) and Peters and Austin (*Passion for Excellence*) portray leadership roles within the same fluid framework of constantly shifting identities.

Catalyst/Motivator: Motivation is ultimately intrinsic, but there are extrinsic strategies that set conditions to invite youngsters into the learning situation, that excite their curiosities and entice them to investigate further. As Dr. Madeline Hunter comments about motivation, "You can lead a horse to water, but you can't make him drink...but you can add salt to his oats." The catalyst/motivator role presumes that "first you've gotta hook them."

For instance, at a recent mind-brain workshop, the trainer captured the curiosity of the participants. By suggesting that following a demonstration on "eye movements" the attendants would be able to "tell if someone was lying," he "hooked" them into the learning situation about to take place, a discussion of neuro-linguistic programming.

Teacher/Educator: Instructional input, teaching methodology, development and implementation of lessons are the components of this role. The teacher demonstrates and models explicit skills as the instructional expert who presents content for student absorption. This role epitomizes the act of teaching as most of us conceive it.

For instance, teaching the skill of classification explicitly, the teacher defines the terms, states the objective, provides instructional input through lecture, media or discussion, structures interaction for students to practice the skills, monitors, reinforces and gives immediate specific feedback.

Facilitator/Coach: When facilitating thinking, the teacher is making it easier. She helps guide, gives specific direction, and coaches with focused attention on particular skill needs. The facilitator/coach is visible, on-the-scene, moving about to observe previously taught skills. The leader in this role senses when *and* when *not* to intercede in the process; she's front and center when needs arise, but she assumes a low profile when the situation seems to be progressing well on its own. In this role, she teaches by guiding the 'book group' as they process a novel; by clarifying the "trouble-shooting" as needed.

Counselor/Cheerleader: This role adheres to the "fluff them up" theory of positive reinforcement for developing student behaviors. It involves active listening, encouragement, 'cheering,' support and meaningful feedback. The counselor/cheerleader role is most often a one-to-one interaction, but there are instances in every classroom when group guidance, direction and support become necessary.

For instance, when a student shifts from an involved participant in discussions to a quiet, uninvolved by-stander, the sensitive teacher notes the variance and finds a private time to talk with the student. Similarly, a student successfully mastering long division is positively reinforced for his success.

Confronter/Disciplinarian: Although this is not a coveted role in the thinking classroom, it is, at times a necessary one. The effective leader handles occasions that call for confrontation, routinely and skillfully as they arise. For instance, during a brainstorming session, one particular student consistently violates the DOVE Guidelines. The effective teacher notes this pattern of behavior and confronts the student appropriately.

Champion: Dr. Benjamin Bloom in *All Our Children Learning*, prods us to "Imagine a classroom learning session which is so powerful that many students have almost total memory of it twenty years later...peak learning experiences...reveal the conditions which are essential to creating them...a charismatic instructor does much to create an atmosphere for peak experiences...(if) the students regard the teacher as one who is communicating some fundamental truth or...some way of viewing phenomena which is both unique and of great moment."

Peters and Waterman advance a similar idea of the necessity of this key figure in *In Search of Excellence*. They note that *without* committed champions, a handful of dedicated people with "know-how," energy, daring and the staying power to implement an idea, the idea dies. Teachers who believe in a 'thinking classroom' display persistence and courage of heroic quality. They are zealous volunteers who present powerful role models to young people. These teachers are 'insanely' good at what they do and what they do is create classrooms that cause students to become intensely involved in their thinking. The role these teachers play is truly one of CHAMPION OF COGNITION.

3. *Cognitive Research*: More than twenty years ago, Mary Budd Rowe introduced the research on wait time. More than 15 years ago, Roger and David Johnson introduced us to the research on cooperative learning. In the past ten years, other researchers including Berliner, Good, Brophy and Resnick have shared the results of their studies about other teaching strategies which marked specific ways to increase student achievement. In the last five years, the research of Resnick, Winograd, Brown and others on cognition, have provided us with an understanding of the reasons why these strategies have worked. This evidence we call cognitive research.

What is cognitive research? It is the study of those effective teaching strategies which help students process information so that they extract meaning from it. It includes what the teacher does to help students understand what they read or hear, solve word problems in math, think critically and creatively in all contents, transfer knowledge and skill to new areas, and think about their thinking in purposeful ways.

Cognitive research has special meaning for the improvement of learning. Because the research has shown us that learning is an active process that contributes to both long term and short term memory, we can no longer argue that learning is the result of rote recall or the artificial linking of bits of information. Rather than place emphasis on drill and practice, the teacher who operates from a cognitive perspective has the assurance that the time spent in processing information through wait-time, higher order thinking discussions and cooperative groups is the more valuable instructional activity for all students. Moreover, there is growing evidence that such processing time is a must for the lower achievers.

Interestingly, some of the best cognitive research has come from the area of reading. When it was noted that poor readers seemed to lack the flexible and fluent attack strategies of the better readers, used ineffective problem solving strategies and spent little time preparing for the reading task, the reading researchers began to look for instructional ways to correct the difficulty. Subsequent research suggested that the teacher could improve reading by cognitive instruction that encouraged the student to draw on the reader's knowledge base, provide the student with new learning strategies for thinking about reading, and refine the student's thinking skills with corrective feedback.

No piece of research has more value to us in this regard than the studies of metacognition. By teaching students to plan purposefully how they intend to think through a reading task and use learned strategies, how they can check or monitor their strategic reading and how they can self evaluate and refine their thinking after the task, the researchers noted how much greater the successes were in reading achievement. More importantly, as students master the PME strategies (planning, monitoring, evaluating), they learn how to control their learning process and take charge of the reading tasks. The more closely we examine cognitive research, the more sharply it brings into focus the importance of taking the time to help students process information. This suggests the value of taking time to provide explicit instruction about thinking skills, teaching of thinking, and the development of student strategies in questioning and visualizing, as precursors of effective thinking about thinking. In specific terms, the cognitive research tells us why wait-time, higher order questions, teacher acceptance, a positive peer climate, cooperative groups, and the other effective teaching strategies worked to increase student achievement. These methods worked because they provided the structure, the time and the expectation for students to think about what they were learning, to make mental connections and to transfer new insights into new situations.

If we take full advantage of cognitive research, it is important that we consider the time trap. Cognitive processing, be it to facilitate concept development in the content or to improve metacognitive strategies for use with course content, takes time. It takes time to structure the strategies and it takes more time for the students to practice. Where do we get the time? There are several possibilities.

(a) Cut down on drill and practice. See short drill and practices only as a preparation for metacognitive discussion or as a check for individual progress after intense metacognitive work.

(b) Save dittos and workbooks for a rainy day. If you check most of your workbooks, they are asking students to *recall* information at least 90% of the time. Instead, take more time to focus students on the key concept of a lesson, plan with them how they are going to apply information processing strategies and thinking skills, monitor their progress, and evaluate how they thought through the task. Instead of covering the pages and answering the recall questions at the end of each chapter, ask higher order questions focused only on the critical concepts.

(c) Keep quiet. Before you begin intense work using effective teaching strategies, tape record several half hours of class time. Count the amount of time you use talking and the amount of talk time for students. The more you talk, the less time is available for students to process. If you are a long winded lecturer, remember that the most attending mind has little chance of absorbing more than 15-20 minutes of straight talk. Select more carefully the most important information and spend at least half the class time to structure student processing of that information.

(d) Re-examine the curriculum and prioritize the most important information. Remember, most standardized tests do not ask for material recall. They test application, analysis, problem solving and other thinking skills. If you are concerned that you can't cover what is "required," recall your days as a "crammer" and what little recall of those facts you now have. If you still want more memory, know that time taken for processing will pay better results in recall and in transfer than many facts crammed for a test.

Most importantly, as students increase their abilities to think effectively, they become more efficient in all their learning. At the minimum, wait-time will give you more attending to questions, more hands raised to process information and more active participation. Cooperative grouping, when correctly used, has shown how it increases achievement as well as student attention to task. Add to this the higher expectations for thinking and the attendant concentration by more students, and you have reduced off task time. Thus, you spend less time correcting student misbehavior and more time with higher order learning. As lower achieving students master the thinking strategies and apply these to all class work, you will see even greater "time savings."

4. **The Methods:** What is it that the teacher does to help students think about their thinking and form their own patterns for thinking? First, the teacher sets the conditions which promote thinking in the classroom. Second, the teacher introduces students to the explicit skills and structures time for the students to practice the skills. As they explore the thinking skills, the teacher uses a variety of techniques that facilitate thinking about thinking.

(a) *The Thinking LOG*: As far back as Leonardo da Vinci, philosophers, poets and inventors kept a daily record of their reactions. They sketched, recorded anecdotes and traced how they were thinking. By using a LOG, students have a private place to play with their ideas, trace patterns of thought and try out, risk free, new ways to develop their thinking.

(b) *The Lead In*: Like leaves from a tree, new ideas sprout from short stems provided by the teacher. The stems prime the pump and help students expand their thinking on a topic. Short stems, such as "I think..." to longer stems are

successful metacognitive starters.

(c) *The Wrap Around*: Allowing each student a turn to comment on an idea helps students share perceptions and appreciate multiple ways to think about a topic.

(d) *Visual Formats*: Graphs, charts, matrices, +/-/? lists, and other visual formats help students structure how they are thinking and provide an easily recalled guide to use in new situations.

(e) *PME*: Questions to prepare, monitor and evaluate one's own thinking guide students through a clear, metacognitive framework. Whether drawn from Bloom or some other taxonomy, these questions make an easy to use tool for checking and improving the quality of one's thinking.

(f) *Creative Problem Solving*: Thinking skills are artificial tools for helping students understand the complexity of the thinking process. When the skills are used as a part of a purposeful process such as CPS, the tools take on a special value especially when facing complex problems. The process reminds us of the tools we have at our disposal so that we can think about which tools will most help us select the best solution.

TEACHING *FOR* THINKING

The teaching for thinking, actively promoting all students to think about the subject matter, falls into two major subdivisions. In the first, the teacher takes time and care to create the conditions which encourage all students to think in the classroom. In the second, the teacher uses a variety of strategies to develop students' attitudes about themselves as problem solvers.

THE CLIMATE *FOR* THINKING:

Many students acquire bad habits and bad attitudes about thinking in the classroom. They expect the teacher to do all the work. The slower the student and the older the student, the more deeply ingrained are these non-thinking attitudes. By high school, where tracking further reinforces non-performance especially among basic students, a teacher might rightfully wonder if any thought is possible. As many teachers using the teaching for thinking strategies can attest, even in those students whose self-beliefs about their own capabilities are the most negative, changes do occur. This is not to say that roses will spring instantaneously from rock, but extra care and extra work will eventually bring change.

What are the most effective tools available if a teacher wants to set the climate for thinking?

1. DISCUSSION GUIDELINES: Fears of ridicule, failure and being wrong prevent many students from active participation in classroom discussion. Over the years, many have learned that school success is a fast track to oblivion. "Don't get caught thinking." The norm is to keep quiet and let the teacher and one or two nerds do the work. To break this norm and to reassure students that they don't have to worry about being shot down by the teacher or their peers, establish guidelines for expected behavior during discussion. Needless to say, these will build upon any rules already in place to promote positive classroom behavior. The DOVE Guidelines are a practical help.

D = Do accept other's ideas. (Avoid criticism and put downs.)

O = Originality is OK. (We need to examine lots of ideas. The way each individual looks at an idea will vary. Share your view.)

V = Variety and vastness of ideas is a start. (After we explore many ideas we can become critical thinkers in search of the best ideas.)

E = Energy and enthusiasm are signs of intelligent and skillful thinkers. (Put your brain to work.)

Post these guidelines and discuss each point. Students can keep a copy of the guidelines in their LOGS.

2. STRUCTURED QUESTIONS FOR DISCUSSION: If students learn to identify the types of questions they are being asked, they will more quickly cue into the type of thinking they are expected to do. Although Benjamin Bloom did not create his cognitive taxonomy for this purpose, categories of his questions can help teachers stimulate thoughtful discussion.

After sharing with the class the DOVE Guidelines, the teacher can initiate a discussion of the guideline's meaning and application by asking sample challenge questions from the taxonomy.

1. In your own words, explain each of the letters.
2. How do you think the ideas of DOVE will help you during classroom discussions?
3. What reason do you think I have for insisting on everyone following these guidelines?
4. What would happen if you had to follow the DOVE Guidelines in every class?
5. Agree or disagree with the idea that it is important to discuss what you are learning in class.

Following the discussion about DOVE, label for the students the type of CHALLENGE questions you asked:

1. Checking for Understanding: "in your own words, explain..."
2. Application: "how can you..."
3. Analysis: "what reason..."
4. Synthesis: "what would happen if..."
5. Evaluation: "agree..."

Post a chart with the DOVE Guidelines and a chart with the CHALLENGE questions on a bulletin board. Let the students know that you expect all to live by the DOVE Guidelines and that you will be asking all to take turns answering the CHALLENGE questions.

3. WAIT-TIME: Asking questions, even in the structured sequence described above, will not accomplish the goal of involving all students in the discussion. With the questions must go the strategic use of what the science researcher, Mary Budd Rowe, called "wait-time."

If there is a single strategy that will yield immediate and dramatic increases in student involvement and interaction, that strategy is "wait-time!" What is wait-time? It is simply: SILENCE! SILENCE! SILENCE! SILENCE! MAGICAL SILENCE! That's it! Silence! Wait 3 - 10 seconds after asking a question. Wait! Just wait! Count silently! Grit your teeth! Pick your fingernail! But wait! And watch what happens. Not only will the length of student response increase, but the probability of clarification, extension, justification and on-task conversation will increase too. Students will begin to listen to each other. Expecting immediate teacher verification and not getting it, classmates nervously will support and defend their own or each other's comments. They will present opposing points of view. They will elaborate and give personal, relevant examples. They will begin to bridge the new concept to past learning and they will demonstrate evidence of THINKING! Just by your silence student participation will noticeably increase.

Although 'wait-time' is not new, it is essential to the 'thinking classroom.' The research documents the effect of 'rapid fire' questioning patterns. Students soon learn that the teacher really isn't interested in thoughtful answers, only quick answers. The effective teacher will communicate that effective thinking by all is a pre-eminent expectation. Thus, that teacher will:

(a) Wait 3 - 10 seconds after each question before calling on any responder.

(b) Wait 3 - 10 seconds after the last response before introducing a new question.

(c) Seek multiple responses to the same question, even when recall is used.

and

(d) Move close to a student who doesn't usually answer.

(e) Ask the question to the class, wait, and then call on the first student.

(f) Establish eye contact and cue the students.

(g) If the student's answer is incomplete, continue questions or paraphrase the response and ask for clarification.

(h) Reinforce the correct response and/or the students' willingness "to hang in there."

4. FORCED RESPONSES: In a BBC program aired on PBS, Private David Jones, a wounded British soldier, faced his class at a private school. His natural order of questions modeled the forced responses. "Suppose," he asked, "that the royalists had won the war. How would history be recorded differently?" The class was silent. Jones waited. Finally, he called on a boy in the last row. "Dobson?" Dobson shook his head. "I don't know, sir."

Jones rephrased the question. Dobson was silent. Jones waited. "Would the winner's point of view predominate?" "I think no, sir." "Why do you say that, Dobson?" "Because, sir, history is history." "What do you mean by that?" "Well, sir, the facts never change." "Anything more?" "Yes, sir, I believe..." and Dobson continued. When he finished, Private Jones said, "That was good thinking, Dobson. That is what you are here for."

Forced responses are specific enabling behaviors which will encourage all students to think actively about *all* questions. "When I ask a question, I expect all to try for their best answer." To assist the *reticent student* the teacher can prompt involvement and break habits of apathy and passivity.

The teacher can encourage responses with techniques that encourage all to participate successfully.

A. Seat Assignments. As often happens in church, persons who want a fast exit sit in the back rows. The devout seek the front pew. Likewise, in school students who don't like class, feel inadequate or prefer to be elsewhere, seek seats or lab stations far removed from the teacher if given the opportunity. The eager students go front and center.

Students learn early in their school careers that teachers attend most to the students with quick answers. To avoid teachers' academic attention, unmotivated students pick the far seats, avoid eye contact, don't raise their hands, and answer as briefly as possible.

To counteract this well-learned, active avoidance, effective teachers will use planned strategies which keep the avoidance close at hand.

(1) Assign seats by performance. Place high performers in the back, low performers to the front.

(2) Move around the room. Be sure avoiders are seated in major paths with quick access.

(3) Let students elect their seats. Each week, place your desk on a different side of the room.

(4) Start multiple responses by calling on students most removed from you.

(5) Use the wraparound calling on each student in turn.

B. Signals. Signals force all students to take a *public position on a question*. If students are sure you will call upon them they will be more inclined to listen to your questions, your instructions, your information. When a signal is accompanied by an attitude on your part that says: "I expect everyone to think, in fact, I'm ecstatic when everyone thinks!", you will find up to a 100% increase in what the students have to say.

There are several practical signals for use in a thinking classroom:

(1) Pre-announced "All Hands." "Think about your *best* answer to my question. When you have an answer, raise your hand. When I see *all hands up*, I'll call on several students for responses." (This leaves open that the "several" may be students who have not raised a hand.)

(2) "Thumbs ups." Pre-teach the signal. When you want a response, ask for thumbs up, sideways or down. Everyone must select and signal one option (post cards, palms out, colored cards, etc...also work).

(3) "Hands up." Pre-teach this signal. When students are working on a task, either together or alone, you will raise your hand to interrupt or end the task. When students see your raised hand, they will end their tasks, raise their own hands, and focus attention to you. After you have explained the process, ask all students to signal with "thumbs up" how well they each understood,

call on one to paraphrase the instructions, gather other responses if needed to have the full answer, reinforce appropriately and end with the entire class practicing "hands up."

(C) *Equal Responsibility to Answer.* Active students who quickly raise hands have the most chance to be called on. In some programs, one or two students can give 95% of all answers as they dialogue with the teacher. The effective teacher calls on all students equally and without a predictable pattern. Thus, every student knows that any question may be his/her question and must be ready to answer. Your dependency on the "quick answering" Suzy will be broken.

There are several ways to build the equal response habit:

(1) Put all names in a hat. Ask a question, pull a name.

(2) Never call a name before a question.

(3) Set a random pattern in your gradebook each week. Check off each name that answers. Work through the whole class.

(4) Use the wraparound with multiple answers. Ask a question; and have each student in turn make a response or say "I pass."

(5) Make your classroom into a Bingo board. Keep numbers in a bingo bin, spin and draw.

In addition to spreading initial questions around the classroom, be sure you spread your extending question. Extending questions ask students to clarify answers, analyze, and evaluate. Usually the most verbal students get this attention. Low participators learn to give superficial grunts because they are never asked to extend.

Some examples of good *extenders* are:

"Can you give me an example of _____?"
"Tell me how..."
"How is that similar to _____?"
"How is that different from _____?"
"What might you do differently when _____?"
"In your own words, _____."

When extending a student response, you will use congruent body language to communicate patience and acceptance of the student's effort to think. When necessary, use non-verbal (head nods, eye contact, smiles) and verbal encouragers to draw the student out. Above all, recall that every student must have the equal chance, the equal responsibility to answer all questions.

(D) *Selective Reinforcement.* The most destructive myth about reinforcement is that every student needs reinforcement for every answer. Rubbish. When a teacher spends half her time saying "good," "wonderful," "excellent" to every student response, she is having no more positive effect than static in a radio opera. At best, the static is blocked out. At worst, it is a waste of time and energy.

Effective reinforcement is selective. The teacher picks a *single accomplishment that a specific student makes* and carefully reinforces that behavior each time it is repeated. For instance, rather than reinforcing all students all of the time for raising hands to answer, the teacher will give special note to the student who has been reticent until this question, "I'm glad that you attempted to answer, Marcia. Your analysis was very complete." When Marcia becomes a regular hand raiser, the teacher will stop the reinforcement for that behavior. In short, the teacher selects reinforcement for specific, appropriate instances of new, *developing behavior.* When students are learning to think, it is best to reinforce the thinking process, not the answer.

5. HURRAHS AND OTHER INDICATORS OF ACCEPTANCE. Driekurs has shown us the importance of acceptance, especially during the tumultuous years when we are forming our self concept. When there is no feedback for expected effort or the only feedback comes as criticism, it is easy to doubt one's own worth. When others give us positive strokes, earnestly for a job well done, we are sparked to continue the effort. Within the thinking classroom, where frequent risk taking is not only encouraged, but expected, it is doubly important that we know our ideas and best efforts at thinking are recognized. A variety of techniques, appropriately selected, will encourage students' positive feelings about the value of their thinking.

Recognition of real effort or meaningful achievement is a basic emotional response sought by all of us. We want to feel appreciated and valued. We need positive strokes from others to signal recognition of that worth. When this recognition is earnest and appropriate, it invariably sparks further effort. Within the thinking classroom, where frequent risk-taking is not only encouraged, but expected, recognition is a must. It sets a non-threatening tone; an accepting climate, where encouragement and regard for all students is a priority.

Techniques that provide recognition can focus on both groups and individuals.

A. *Hurrahs!*

The 'hurrah' is a wonderful, often spontaneous action to signal recognition of another or to energize the group as a whole.

(1) *North County Hurrah*

An enthusiastic, but silent waving of the hands overhead, in shivering fashion, constitutes the North Country hurrah.

(2) *Standing "O"*

Place both arms overhead in a classic ballet position creating a "standing ovation,"

or the standing "O."

(3) *Give A Hand*

To give a hand, place the right arm across the chest and over the opposite shoulder. Then "pat" yourself on the back for a job well-done.

B. *Encouraging Statements:* Encouragement occurs before the event: praise comes after. You encourage a five year old to balance on her two wheeler as you push/hold her down the street. When finally, she takes off, peddling frantically without your steady hand (and sore back!), you praise her accomplishment. Encouragement communicates your belief in the student's capability. "I know you can do this next problem. It's difficult, but you have done tougher problems correctly."

C. *Post-it Note:* A brief, specific, positive note of praise "posted" on a student paper or desk is a 'warm fuzzy' that is usually saved and reread many times. It also models communication through writing.

D. *Equal Help:* Help is often construed by students as something they receive outside the classroom, after school. It is shunned because student norms have dictated for eons against seeking help. Helping is easily *seen* as "brown nosing." Some teachers even see students seeking help as manipulators. "Oh, she's just trying to get my attention." or "He's trying to get a better grade." Far worse, some students avoid help because they believe getting help has something to do with being bright or dumb. "If anybody knew I couldn't do those problems, well..." As a teacher, you must help students overcome this fear by encouraging your students to seek help.

Help starts in the classroom. If a teacher does more than pour information into empty student heads for regurgitation (A recent study showed that in many classrooms, up to 89% of the time is spent this way!), the teacher will provide structured discussion time. That time will help the teacher analyze what student "thinking" difficulties are and *help* the student. If any student is having difficulty *applying* knowledge (i.e. basic math skills to word problems), transferring knowledge (i.e. making generalizations), seeing relationships (i.e. how is a literary character similar to current government leaders), the teacher will help the student with the thought processes. The teacher will not worry about "how much time this is taking away from my lesson plan."

Such help may come in guided individual practice as the teacher walks around the classroom and monitors especially those students who might have difficulty, in cooperative group reviews or in all class discussions in which mistakes are analyzed and corrected.

Most importantly, all students, especially the learners who have the most learning difficulties, will *perceive* that the teacher does provide equal help for all.

E. *Dignifying Responses:* Every student will not answer every question appropriately. Rather than embarrass a student by put downs ("That's a stupid answer."), sarcasm ("You might try studying."), guilt trips ("Don't you realize what you are doing to yourself?"), or personal insults ("You are dumb, aren't you?"), an effective teacher will dignify the responses by noting the correct part of the answer ("Tom, you're correct about the number of accidents recorded in 1985."), and ask other students to build on that ("And, who can clarify the major causes?"). If the student is totally off on a single right answer, at least acknowledge the effort *with* sincerity. You may avoid this trap, however, by *always* seeking multiple answers and then selecting the correct answer. For instance, if you asked students to solve this word problem, you would dignify responses this way. "I'm going to list several answers on the board." As you get each answer say "Thank You" and record it. "Now I'm going to compare answers." Select but don't identify the correct answer and work through the problem to show the correct process. Ask the students with the incorrect process/answer to show you what they could correct in their own example. Reinforce them for identifying the change because you "have caught them thinking."

F. *Focusing on Concerns:* Just as teacher may come to school with concerns and problems which make it hard to focus on the day's task, so too, students may be hindered from their day's task of learning. Without turning every class into a counseling session, the effective teacher helps students with these concerns.

(1) *Academic Concerns:* Homework assignments, questions about yesterday's class discussion, a due reading assignment - each can block a student's concentration on the here and now lesson.

(2) *Personal Concerns:* A family death, finances, lost materials, a stolen bike may dominate a student's feelings as the day begins.

The easiest approach is the preventive approach. At the beginning of the day, or the start of a class, the teacher can ask for Comfort, Concerns and Continuity: "What issues, problems, or concerns are you experiencing which will keep you from giving full attention to today's lessons?" Sometimes, students will identify that they are worried about a coming special assignment or test; other times, it may be forgotten lunch money, a medical appointment. More often, there are no responses to the 3 C's, but the effort is appreciated.

In deciding how to answer concerns, the teacher must make several decisions. The first is centered on the issue what is best for the student, the second on what is best for the class and the third is based on time.

a. *The Student.* Is a full answer needed now? or can it be saved for a private tete-a-tete? If the latter is true, indicate a short answer now and a complete answer at a specific time and place. "Kate, my short answer is that all buses will leave at 5 P.M. If you need a longer explanation, see me at the door on the way to lunch."

b. *The Class.* Will the entire class benefit from the public response? Is it a general concern that needs a public response? If so, decide on how much time you will need to allot.

c. *The Time.* All effective discussions are a question of time. The formal concerns session is best limited to five minutes. Obviously, a major concern that involves many students will need more time.

A Special Note: It is important to recall that concerns are a feeling issue. Therefore, it is best to focus on the feeling, not the event. If you provide only solutions to a problem, without checking for a changed feeling tone, the concern wil remain. If the student's feelings are sufficiently strong and not resolved, you can bet no thinking will occur that day!

Obviously, a formal five minute, 3C session at the beginning of the day will not eliminate concerns or issues that might arise in a day. The 3C session is designed to give students a comfortable time to bring up issues. As issues arise during the day, you can help the student decide whether the concern can wait until the next morning or must be resolved at once. As with concerns identified in the A.M. session, you will want to (a) reflect on the feeling, (b) focus the concern with a "what do you want," (c) and check that the feelings behind the concern are resolved.

G. *Talking Up:* A crucial variable in each of the behaviors described in this unit is *tone.* Tone of voice, as in "Don't speak to me in that tone of voice!" is subtle. A slight inflection can change a warm praise into a sarcastic bite. The effective teacher communicates with a warm, business-like tone. Sarcastic and sardonic tones which have the purpose of putting a student down or hurting the student are unnecessary and ineffective. While "cuts" may silence a student for a moment, more likely they will silence a student for a long, long time. More effective than talking down, is talking up...finding the positive thing to say to each student.

How long you will have to work with any given class to set the conditions for thinking will depend on the learning history and the personalities of each class. If you are in high school or junior high, the time variable may even depend on the period of the day. What you try with your first period class may differ drastically from what works sixth period. It will also depend on how students are grouped in your school, their past experiences and parental attitudes.

Given your success with setting the conditions for thinking you can increase the challenge to think. By increasing the students' familiarity with higher order questions and by asking more and more extending questions of all the students, you will improve their discussion skills and promote greater quality in how they think about your course content. BUT...BEWARE!!! You will also increase the amount of time you spend on each lesson.

EXTENDING STUDENT THINKING: (MORE QUESTIONS)

As you spend more time with discussion in your course, you and the students can refine question asking skills. They will soon discover that there are many words which structure responses to questions. When asked in a sequence the question cues resemble the rungs of a ladder. The "lower" questions are easy to reach; the higher require more complex thinking.

F Evaluation

E Synthesis

D Analysis

C Application

B Comprehension

A Recall

(A) Can students recall factual information?

    (1) A memorized list (short).
    (2) A memorized definition.
    (3) A memorized sequenced list by time, by importance, and by anagram.

(B) Can students understand concepts?

    (1) Translate into own words.
    (2) Paraphrase simple statements.
    (3) Explain in own words "what this means to me."

(C) Can students apply a concept?

    (1) Relate the day-to-day use of the concept.
    (2) Describe uses of the idea in school or home situations.

(D) Can students analyze a concept?

    (1) How object is like another? (physical example)
    (2) How the objects are different?
    (3) How object is like another? (abstraction)
    (4) How to classify objects?

(E) Can students think creatively?

    (1) Make a change in an idea?
    (2) Predict what would happen if you...?
    (3) Forecast consequences?

(F) Can students evaluate?

    (1) Tell why they like _____?
    (2) Explain which is best _____?
    (3) Judge which is most _____?
    (4) Decide _____?

There are innumerable question keys at each level. Here is a chart for your reference.

Sample Questions and Key Words to use in Developing Questions

I. **Knowledge** (Eliciting factual answers, testing recall and recognition)

Who	Where	Describe	Which One	Label
What	How	Define	Name	List
Why	How much	Memorize	Point Out	Reproduce
When	Recall	Select		

II. **Comprehension** (Translating, interpreting, and extrapolating)

State In Your Own Words	Locate	Indicate
What Does This Mean	Give an Example	Tell
Select The Definition	Condense This Paragraph	Translate
State In One Word	Explain What is Happening	Outline
What Part Doesn't Fit	Explain What Is Meant	Summarize
Read The Graph Table This Represents	What Restrictions Would You Add	Select
Explain	What Exceptions Are There	Match
Define	What Are They Saying	Identify

III. **Application** (Using in situations that are new, unfamiliar to students)

How Would You Use	Make A Lesson	Show How
What Is The Use For	Demonstrate How	Apply
Tell What Would Happen	If...How	Construct
Choose The Statements That Apply		Explain
Tell How Much Change There Would Be		Identify

IV. **Analysis** (Breaking down into parts, relating parts to the whole)

Distinguish	What Inconsistencies, Fallacies
Diagram	What Literacy Form Is Used
Similar	What Persuasive Technique
Like	What Relationship Between
Chart	What Is The Function Of
Plan	What's Fact, Opinion
Dissect	State The Point Of View Of
Contrast	What Ideas Justify Conclusion
Cause For	What Assumptions
Arrange	What Motive Is There
Separate	What Conclusions
Conclude	Make A Distinction
Outline	What Is The Premise
Different	Implicit In The Statement Is The Idea Of
	What's The Theme, Main Idea, Subordinate Idea
Graph	The Least Essential Statements Are
Classify	What Does Author Believe, Assume
Compare	Deduce
Differentiate	What Statement Is Relevant, Extraneous To,
Reason For	Related To, Not Applicable
Investigate	Categorize

V. Synthesis (Combining elements into a pattern not clearly there before)

Write	Build	Blend
Create	Make A Film	How Would You Test
Tell	Solve	Propose An Alternative
Make	Make Up	Solve The Following
Do	Dance	Formulate A Theory
Choose	Ad	How Else Would You
Hypothesize	What if	What Different If Predict
Plan	Design	State A Rule
Compose	Develop	Imagine
Combine	Invent	Infer
Estimate	Forecast	Predict
Invent	Construct	

VI. Evaluation (Judging according to some set of criteria and stating why)

Appraise	Judge	Criticize	Defend
Editorialize	Decide	Rate	Value
Which Is Best	Verify	Dispute	Grade
Choose Why	Evaluate	Find The Errors	

What Fallacies, Consistencies, Inconsistencies Appear

Which Is More Important, Moral, Better, Logical, Valid, Appropriate, Inappropriate

A social studies lesson using higher order questions might look like this:

The Causes of The Black Plague

I. **Anticipatory Set:** (3 minutes) Describe to the students what happened last year when half the school had the flu.

II. **Input:** (20 minutes)

  1. Define the word "plague"
  2. Give examples of various plagues.
  3. Lecture on the Black Plague

      A. Causes
      B. Effects on Society
      C. Major Statistics

III. **Discussion:** (15 minutes)

  1. In your own words, describe the causes and effects of the Black Plague. (Comprehension)
  2. What would result today if the Black Plague struck this school? (Application)
  3. Graph the death tolls for three counties struck by the plague. (Analysis)
  4. If you were the county medical doctor, how would you help a plague victim? (Synthesis)
  5. Defend the people who wouldn't help the plague victims. (Evaluation)

The same procedure will work with stories. Primary students might discuss a fairy tale.

THE THREE LITTLE PIGS

I. **Anticipatory Set:** (3 minutes) Ask the students to predict what would happen to them if their house was blown away.

II. **Input:** (5 minutes) Read the story "The Three Little Pigs."

III. **Discussion:** (15 minutes)

1. Recall key facts. (Recall)

2. In your own words, tell what happened to the pigs. (Understanding)

3. What would you do if a bad person knocked on your door? (Application)

4. How were the pigs' houses different? (Analysis)

5. What would have happened if a policeman were present? (Synthesis)

6. Explain why you think the pigs were good thinkers or bad thinkers. (Evaluation)

IV. **Closure:** Check predictions made earlier in class.

All children need time to reflect on information. The more we know about metacognition, the thinking about thinking, the more we recognize the importance of structuring time for students to think about the information we provide. Yes, this will mean less information and more discussion. When we provide that time by asking well structured questions, we are teaching *for* thinking.

In *Catch Them Thinking,* we have integrated the many strategies which promote more skillful thinking in the classroom. The more of these strategies you have in your repertoire the more you will succeed in promoting more skillful thinking by all your students.

TEACHING *OF* THINKING

Dr. Barry Bayer is the leading advocate for teaching explicit thinking skills which he calls, "the teaching of thinking." In this approach, the teacher identifies 4 - 8 thinking skills which are already included in the subject matter. For instance, classification is taught implicitly in Biology, problem solving is implicit in math word problems, attributing in character analysis of a novel. Although the best students are able to grasp these thinking skills which are buried in the content, most students seldom recognize or master them. As a result, when they have to use the skills without teacher direction, the students can only guess at what to do. Beyer argues that formal instruction in explicit thinking skills will give all students the tools to do more skillful thinking.

What goes into this formal instruction? First, there is a formal lesson design. As we have used it in the 50 strategic lessons, the design includes:

1. **A FOCUS ACTIVITY** This is the advanced organizer or anticipatory set that Rowe's research showed to be so important in helping students focus their attention on the topic at hand. In this case, the activity will focus concentration on a specific thinking skill such as comparing or predicting.

2. **THE LESSON OBJECTIVE** This will spell out to students what they will learn in this lesson. It is important that the teacher communicate the objective, both by sight and by sound, to the students before the lesson and as much as necessary during the lesson. Effective teachers follow the adage: "This is what I am going to teach you. This is what I am teaching you. This is what I did teach you." As often as students ask "What are we doing?", that is how often it is necessary to reinforce the objective.

3. **INPUT** Students need solid information about the thinking skill. If it is their first introduction, they will need a clear definition with synonyms, an explanation of when and how the thinking skill is used, an easy way to remember the mental operations used in the thinking process and a demonstration of how one used the skill in a thinking task. The task selected should be one that makes it easy for them to focus on the key mental operations of the skill without confusing the thinking process with the course content. For instance, biology students would best learn classification by grouping types of clothes or popular music. After having grasped the classifying rules and procedures, they can apply the rules to botany and zoology.

For students who have a working knowledge of the thinking skill, a more inductive approach will benefit. Rather than give the definition and operations to the students, you might set up an experiment which requires them to think through the task or problem solve. Then you would use questions to help the class generalize a definition and list the operations they used. For instance, in social studies, you might provide the class with data that indicates a number of social trends. From the data, the class would predict future events. When they have completed the task, you would review how they solved the problem and develop acceptable rules for making logical predictions.

4. **STRUCTURED ACTIVITY** Under your close supervision, the class would practice or apply the information they had received about the thinking skill. This important step is too often overlooked. In fact, it is as important for you to structure the practice, observe what students do and give corrective feedback as it is for you to give them the information about the thinking skill. Until they have the opportunity to use the information and refine its use, they have no skill. If a teacher is not going to take this practice and feedback time, she might as well *not* take the time to fill the students' heads with useless definitions, synonyms and uses of the thinking skill.

5. **METACOGNITIVE DISCUSSION** Once

the students have had the opportunity to try out the skill, they need the opportunity to process what they have done. This mental processing, thinking about their thinking, we call "metacognition." This is the tool that reading researchers now are able to tell us helps pull the isolated skills into a holistic understanding. Without the time to think about thinking, the chances are very high that students will not tie the pieces together and find meaning in what they are thinking about. Without this meaning, they will have very little chance to retain or to transfer what they have learned to content areas.

As a method for promoting metacognition, the stems ("I think..." "I wonder..." "I learned...") are an easy first step. Using Bloom's Taxonomy with the higher level questions focused on the thinking accomplished in the structured task ("How might you use the predicting skill in your job?" "What would happen if you used the 5 step problem solving model...") is a second method. A third approach is the PME model: planning, monitoring and evaluating how we think.

Planning your thinking

1. What is your thinking goal? Is it achievable? Believable? Conceivable?

2. How will you think to get there?

3. How will you sequence your thinking tasks?

4. What problems will occur?

5. How will you overcome these problems?

6. What will give you the most trouble in your thinking?

7. Predict what will happen...?

8. How will you know you have succeeded in this thinking task?

Monitoring your thinking

1. Where are you in the sequence of mental operations?

2. What surprises did you discover? How did you handle the surprise in your thinking? What did you decide to do?

3. What mistakes did you make in your thinking? How did you adjust? Recover?

4. What have you learned new about your thinking patterns?

5. What have you reinforced about what you do well?

Evaluating your thinking

1. What did you think about?

2. What operations/skills did you use?

3. If you did this thinking task over, what would you do differently?

4. What did you do well? Goal/Skill use?

5. What are you unsure about?

6. How accurate was your thinking?

7. How precise was your thinking?

8. How fluent was your thinking?

9. How flexible was your thinking?

F. **CLOSURE.** Before ending a lesson on a specific thinking skill, it is advisable to check carefully to ascertain how well students have mastered the skill. If necessary, repeat input, structured activity and the metacognitive discussion. You may want to have students explain the definitions and operations, change the activity and use different questions. When you have ample evidence that at least 80% mastery is present, move to the lesson closure. At its best, an effective closure will help students key on the critical learnings about the skill in a way that will encourage strong retention for future use. At the worst, closure will be a quiz which communicates that the skill can be filed away forever.

The formal lesson, however, is only the first step in the explicit instruction of the thinking skill. Once students have a mastery of what the skill is and how to use it, they are ready for transfer lessons into one or more subjects. The transfer lesson will follow the same design principles as the introductory lesson. The teacher will make instructional decisions about which components (focus, input, etc.) to include and which to pass over in each transfer lesson. For instance, the classification transfer lesson to Biology may require no more than a review of the introductory lesson. The review would serve as focus and input. Very quickly, the students would begin a classification activity using 40 words provided on the overhead. After a brief metacognitive discussion, they might start a second classifying activty, using lab equipment. Each time, they would think about how they were classifying and find ways to improve that thinking skill. Ultimately, the teacher might challenge them to classify objects that have no relationship to Biology to test their grasp of the classifying skill itself.

These components are not selected by accident. The more we learn about the secrets of cognition, the more apparent it becomes that each piece contributes to the quality of thinking about the content. The secret of success in learning springs from the student's ability to take information, and cognitively integrate the new with the old. This leads to meaning. Some students intuitively structure meaning. Each piece, like the components of a computer menu, plays an important part in helping all students learn how to structure the pieces into a meaningful whole. Given solid instruction, visual formats, clues and intense practice, each gets the chance to integrate the single skills into a personally meaningful mental construct.

The danger inherent in the teaching of thinking is that the discrete skills remain single and isolated. There is little value in this approach if students are not given the opportunities to practice and transfer the thinking skills into the course content and to integrate the single skills into a cognitive whole.

In *Catch Them Thinking*, there are 50 strategic lessons which use this model. These lessons are meant as introductions to each of the explicit skills. In the Practice and Transfer section, you will find suggestions for how to extend the skills into a variety of course contents.

TEACHING *WITH* THINKING

Roger and David Johnson, two brothers who work cooperatively at the University of Minnesota, have researched the values of cooperative, competitive and individualistic learning in the classroom. Their studies, most recently elaborated in ASCD's *Circles of Learning*, argue for the superiority of cooperative groups over competitively and individualistically organized classrooms. When properly implemented, cooperative groups are especially powerful in promoting thinking and problem solving in the classroom.

In the *Catch Them Thinking* lessons, we have adapted cooperative group methodology as the key to many of the structured activities. Classroom teachers who piloted many of these lessons preferred the cooperative group strategies for several reasons. First, the small groups required more total involvement in the thinking tasks. It was very easy for even the more shy or the more resistant learner to get involved. The teacher could observe more student thinking. The teachers caught more students thinking aloud. Secondly, the cooperative groups provided the less skilled thinkers with models and peer coaching. With the emphasis on cooperation rather than competition that produces winners and losers, a more positive classroom climate developed. Thirdly, as the groups became more skilled in their cooperation, the teacher was freed to concentrate less on management and more on helping individuals develop and apply the thinking skills. Fourth, the teachers felt more comfortable with the amount of cognitive processing that cooperative groups allowed.

Each of the lessons is designed for cooperative groups of 3 - 5 students. When organizing the groups we suggest that you follow these guidelines.

1. **ABANDON THE BLUEBIRDS** Do not use homogenous groups for these activities. Instead, mix the groups so that there is a balance of high performers and low performers in each group. In the first few months, rotate groups so that there is a constant variation allowing most students to work with most other students. Don't allow student self selection, but work for constant mixes of male/female, task directed/socializers, majority/minority and so on.

2. **BALANCE THE TIME** Some of the tasks have time limits. Other tasks you will have to judge for yourself. When you see one or two groups finish a task, announce "two more minutes" and stick to it. Some of the lessons will take thirty - forty minutes; others several hours. For younger students, break the lessons into several parts and sequence the parts over several days. For the older students, you may want to do the lesson and the transfer lessons over two or three weeks. Keep groups intact through a lesson.

3. **MOVE FURNITURE QUIETLY** Each lesson may call for two or three different arrangements of desks. All-class discussions are facilitated by a circle or half moon. Input requires students to face you and the board. Small groups will function with desks drawn close enough for low voice conversation, but removed from other small circles to avoid distractions. Model for students how to move the desks quietly and reinforce that behavior. Expect that desks are rearranged by the students for the next class.

4. **PREPARE MATERIALS BEFORE CLASS** Many of the lesson activities call for newsprint and markers. Have these ready for quick and easy distribution. Expect that all materials will be returned before the end of the task.

5. **ASSIGN TASK ROLES** Each student in the group should have a specific role and understand the responsiblities of that role. The most basic roles are the leader who keeps the group on task, the recorder who uses the newsprint or worksheet, and the timekeeper who watches the clock and checks task progress. Other roles, such as the observer who records and gives feed-

back to the group on how well members cooperate and the materials manager who makes sure that the group has all its materials, may also be needed. When assigning roles, try to ensure rotation so that all students learn all tasks. Selecting roles can be a creative endeavor. For instance, find the person who lives farthest from school, is tallest, is wearing the most of a color, has the most letters in the last name, etc. When that person is identified in each group, assign a role. then assign the other roles in an equally random way.

6. **EXPLAIN THE TASK** Give clear, specific instructions. Especially in the beginning of the year, check for understanding by asking one or more students to explain your instructions in their own words. When necessary, ask other students to explain for you, especially when giving examples of key terms.

7. **STRUCTURE POSITIVE GOAL INTERDEPENDENCE** Reinforce to each group that they have a team goal and must work cooperatively. They will sink or swim together. The final product is a group product.

8. **STRUCTURE INDIVIDUAL ACCOUNTABILITY** The group is responsible for making sure that every individual masters the thinking skill. Each individual will be expected to know key concepts, especially the mental menu and the skill definition.

9. **SPECIFY AND OBSERVE DESIRED BEHAVIORS** Students should know which intelligent behaviors you are looking for. At the minimum, this will mean that they follow DOVE, participate actively in the discussion and carry out individual roles. As the groups improve, carry a check sheet and record data that you can share later with the students. The check sheet will include such behaviors as contributing ideas, asking questions, actively listening, expressing support and acceptance, summarizing, giving positive direction to the group, encouraging others to participate, clarifying, affirming and testing options.

10. **SET CLEAR CRITERIA FOR SUCCESS** Provide examples to model high quality products which you expect from the group work. Make it possible for all to reach the criteria without penalizing others.

Initially students may find it difficult to maintain on task behavior when in small groups. However if you approach the groupings with care and follow the guidelines, you will find that they soon become the most productive learning time in the day. The time you give to preparation and practice of group behavior in the beginning of the year, you will quickly make up within a few months. If breakdowns occur the best care is to stop the group, discuss the difficulty and encourage students to refine the classroom rules. You will find that they value the group learning so highly that they will police their own problems and return promptly to the challenge of thinking.

MRS. POTTER

TEACHING *ABOUT* THINKING

The Teaching About Thinking, what is properly called "metacognition" or "going beyond thinking," may be the most powerful and important of all the approaches. First, it is the glue that binds all the pieces. Isolated skills, no matter how well taught, have limited influence on the quality of thinking. Metacognitive activity encourages the skillful thinker to make the connections with conscious effort. Secondly, metacognition is a critical part of the process whereby the student masters any of the thinking skills.

After direct instruction of an explicit skill the student reviews the mental operations in the newly acquired skill before additional practice. After the practice, the student may examine the same operations and seek ways to refine their use. Thirdly, if the teacher is adept at asking metacognitive questions and if the peer climate is safe and secure, the teacher will extend student thinking beyond higher level questions with metacognitive questions.

As the research on cognition indicates, cognitive processing is one of the most important learning tools a student possesses. It is not enough to absorb information. The student must take the time to make meaning from the facts and figures. In a hurry up society full of mad hatters running around shouting "I'm late. I'm late for a very important date," students are more ready to adapt to the expectation for speed. How easy it is to get the message that a slow response is a dumb response!

To break the Mad Hatter Syndrome, the skilled teacher will use any and all of the tools at her disposal to promote cognitive processing: wait-time, higher order questioning, peer acceptance, cooperative problem solving, explicit lessons, active mental involvement and the high expectation that all students think about what they are thinking.

Cognitive processing is integral to every thinking classroom. It happens because the skilled teacher makes it happen. Each and every lesson, whether it is an explicit thinking skill or not, is enhanced when the lesson design incorporates processing time.

There are three teachable moments when a cognitive processing can enhance a lesson: the set or focus activity, the metacognitive discussion or the checking for understanding, and the closure.

1. **THE ANTICIPATORY SET** Rowe's early research called this "the advanced organizer." Madeline Hunter popularized the label "anticipatory set." The word "organizer" more accurately describes the cognitive behavior that occurs in the student's mind when the teacher focuses the student's attention on the lesson's aim. The organizer helps the student go to short term memory to review related material, fit it into the new context and make the needed connections. While many lessons will need only a short set to help the students with the needed mental organization, the skilled teacher will allow sufficient time and assistance for the students to acquire the needed focus. At no time in the lesson is the adage "haste makes waste" more appropriate than during "the set" when students, each at an individual rate, are organizing for learning.

2. **CHECKING FOR UNDERSTANDING/ DISCUSSION** It is absurd to believe that simple signals can give clues to how well a student comprehends even the most simple instructions. Mass checking is the surest way to kill thinking in the classroom. Skilled checking will expect that all children take the time to think about their thinking and that the teacher will take the time to elicit sample responses. She will use all she knows about seeking multiple responses, attending to the perceived low performers and waiting after her thought producing questions. And, as the occasion demands, she will check for application, analysis and evaluation. When working with an explicit teaching skill, she will take enough time to guide the discussion into a complete cognitive processing of the skill itself, especially as the skill relates to other

learned thinking skills and the application of the skill to real life situations.

3. **CLOSURE.** Cognitive processing is integral to successful learning. If we consider each lesson as having three parts, "what" and "so what" and "now what," we can examine the importance of closure. In the "what," students give evidence that they understand the critical pieces of the lesson. Can they put the objective in their own words, using information acquired during the lesson? If not, why go on?

In the "so what," students must stop to make personal application. They link the new learning to past learnings, associated thoughts and feelings and lock it into the larger contexts of the course and their own lives. In essence, this is the time that each discovers the meaning of what was taught.

In the "now what," the student makes the information come alive as he investigates applications and projects the new learning into future situations. He is encouraged to make abstract ideas practical in a context that he can understand. This brings his thinking into final focus or closure.

The "what," "so what" and "now what" challenge students to internalize what they are learning. Whether the teacher uses questions from Bloom, Gallagher or Taba matters little. That the teacher takes the time with some set of higher order questions matters a great deal. Without this time, retention, motivation and transfer will limp along, even disappear as the students read the message, "covering more material faster is more important than understanding any material well." With that, we are back to Pygmalion.

At whichever point you decide to process how students are thinking, there are several guidelines which can help:

1. When asking process questions, avoid questions that students can answer with a "yes" or "no" or a one word answer. Note in the strategies, we have asked only open ended questions. Even when we ask for a report on what students learned or did in cooperative groups, we structure the questions for multiple responses.

2. All information questions are best followed by a series of higher order questions. The questions focus on the critical content or key concept of the lesson. If the lesson focuses on a thinking skill, the questions focus on that skill.

3. Ask only one question at a time. Tell students that you will only ask each question once and that you intend to wait for many responses. If a student does not understand your question, encourage the student to ask you to clarify the question. Don't fall into the repeater trap and please don't answer your own question.

4. Ask extending questions as often as you decide necessary. This is especially important when you feel unsure of a student's meaning or you feel that the response could be more specific.

5. Practice your wait-time. When you are using questions to structure metacognition, it is most important that you signal your respect for time to think.

6. To increase student involvement, especially the first times you ask metacognitive questions, have them write first and then share responses. The wraparound in the beginning is also helpful. Allow students to say "I pass" at any time. If passing becomes a problem, go back and examine what you can do to make the climate more safe.

7. Vary the techniques you use to get students to process what they have learned. In the strategies, we have used the LOG, the wraparound, lead ins, higher order questions on the Bloom model and creative activities (collages, essays, stories, etc.) in a variety of ways to focus on the skill of each lesson. You might want to change any of the suggestions such as using "What," "So What," "Now What,"

"Mrs. Potter's Questions" or some other sequences of your choosing.

8. Always address processing questions to the entire class. This communicates that all must think about the question. Encourage the fast hand wavers to take more time to think. After all have had the think time, call on your first choice.

9. Encourage active listening. We placed the "pre-skills" first among the strategies so that you can teach students, if necessary, how to listen to each other. If you find some students who are not listening to the processing done by their peers, you may want to ask those students to paraphrase what others are saying before they give their own answers.

10. Avoid the "why" questions such as "Why did Columbus sail to America?" Instead ask: "Why do you think...?" This avoids the one right answer syndrome and forces students to make personal connections. In addition, it leaves you ready to follow up with "What proof will you give?" when students are making wild assumptions.

11. Model acceptance. Overmodel it. As each student responds, keep strong eye contact, nod at key points and occasionally summarize key points. Don't interrupt and don't put the student down. If the logic is faulty, has incorrect information or false assumptions, use your clarifying and extending skills to help the student discover the mistake. If you have asked the question so that the students must give an opinion (Why do you think...?), you will find that students will have little difficulty accepting a redirection for the sake of logic.

12. Acknowledge skillful thinking. Avoid praise for its own sake. This will keep you from sounding like a broken record to the students (good...good...good...wonderful...good...), but do indicate in very specific terms that a student has displayed skillful thinking. "I appreciate the detail you gave as your proof, Mary."

13. Encourage students to answer each other, not you. Tell them that you will be responsible to be where you can hear, but that they should talk to the class. As discussions begin, encourage students to look at all responses from a variety of viewpoints. For instance, after a student has answered a question in the positive, ask who holds the opposite point of view. Or after one student completes a statement, ask for a show of hands. How many agree? How many disagree? Solicit responses from both sides.

14. Encourage students to focus, accept and draw each other out. Demonstrate how they can use body language to show focus and discuss how it feels to have someone pay full attention to you. Teach them a few ways to draw out a response (clarifying questions, paraphrasing, etc.)

15. Label student thinking. When you hear a student analyzing, acknowledge that. When you notice that a student is classifying, note it to the student. If the student's classifying needs refinement, suggest changes.

16. Recognize that there are many chances to encourage metacognition. When students are reading, discuss the thinking skills they are applying. For instance, when they have to search out clues and "read between the lines," recall inferring.

17. Note that the main difference between the cognitive processing of a content such as the "origin of the Civil War" or "a prime number" and the metacognitive processing of one's thinking is the focus. The processing of one's thinking is doubly dependent on how well you set the safe climate, maintain the conditions and hold the students to your high expectations for thinking about thinking. It helps students if you process concepts at least once a day. As they become used to processing concepts, you will find their readiness to metacognate will increase.

18. As students become more skilled in how

they process both the concepts of your course and their own thinking, you will experience that metacognition will "eat up" time. Once you find the students are comfortable with metacognition, you must plan more precisely when to cut off the discussions and when to move on. The LOG can help. Bring students to closure by inviting them to reflect in the LOG.

19. Grades. At some point, the question will arise. As soon as it does you will find yourself a Catch 22 victim. If you must grade how well students think, try these suggestions.

   a. Test for knowledge of a thinking skill (definition, uses, operations).

   b. Give at least three application questions of the skill. Check for the student's ability to think through the operations.

   c. Have students self-rate improvement in their intellectual behaviors and provide proof from their own experience. (i.e. increased flexibility, fluency, creative problem solving, etc.)

The preference is that you not grade student thinking. Instead, look for improved intellectual behavior that you can reinforce skillful thinking and give positive feedback to the student.

In the fifty lessons that follow, we have synthesized the best practice of effective teaching to produce more skillful thinkers. Classroom teachers piloted each lesson making adaptions for age, class size and background. Only those evaluated as most effective were included. We are sharing these with you so that you too can structure your classroom and "catch" your students thinking.

TRANSFER: THE CREATIVE CONNECTION

All teaching is for transfer. All learning is for transfer. The mission of the thinking classroom is to extend learning; to bridge the old and the new; to lead students toward relevant transfer and use across academic content and into life situations.

In some cases, the transfer of learning is obvious because the learned skills seem close to the skill situation in which it is transferred. For example, when teaching "supermarket math," price comparisons, making change etc., the life situation "hugs" the learning situation.

Learning in the school situation can seem far removed or remote from the transfer across content or into life. For example, a high school student spends a great deal of time and energy staring at, memorizing and using the Periodic Table of Elements. However, unless the student is destined for a scientific career in which frequent reference to and deep understanding of the table is essential, it is difficult for the student to feel that the learning is really useful in his life. Does one really need to know that AU is the symbol for gold?

Most students do not "see" the connection between the rigors of learning the elements and the similar rigors of visualizing, practicing and memorizing other material. Few students note that the analytical skills used in "reading" the table of elements are similar to the critical thinking used in analyzing other charts or graphs. Seldom are students aware that the patterns evident in the table of elements set a model for searching for patterns in other phenomena. The transfer here is remote; it is obscure. The student needs explicit instruction in making connections.

In these situations, teachers can help kids make relevant transfer through mediation or "bridging" strategies.

TRANSFER: THE CREATIVE CONNECTION
(Mediation Strategies That Bridge Learning)

Transfer Strategy #1: Setting Expectations
SET EXPECTATIONS for transfer. Elicit examples of when the information, skill or concept is used in other content or in life situations. Ask students how they might use this new learning.

Transfer Strategy #2: Reflecting Metacognitively
REFLECT ON YOUR TRANSFER LEVEL. Ask yourself, "which of these birds am I?"

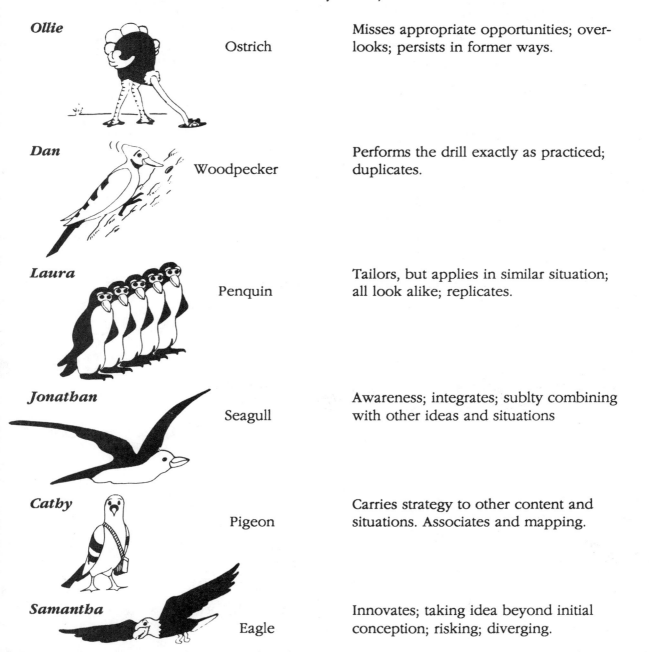

Ollie
Ostrich
Misses appropriate opportunities; over-looks; persists in former ways.

Dan
Woodpecker
Performs the drill exactly as practiced; duplicates.

Laura
Penquin
Tailors, but applies in similar situation; all look alike; replicates.

Jonathan
Seagull
Awareness; integrates; sublty combining with other ideas and situations

Cathy
Pigeon
Carries strategy to other content and situations. Associates and mapping.

Samantha
Eagle
Innovates; taking idea beyond initial conception; risking; diverging.

Transfer Strategy #3: Making Connections
USE BRIDGING STATEMENTS such as:

OVERLOOKING
Think of an instance when the skill or strategy would be inappropriate.
"I would not use _____ when _____
_____."

DUPLICATING
Think of an "opportunity passed" when you could have used the skill or strategy.
"I wish I'd known about _____ when _____
I could've_____."

REPLICATING
Think of an adjustment that will make your application of _____
_____ more relevant.
"Next time I'm gonna _____
_____."

INTEGRATING
Think of an analogy for the skill or strategy.
"_____ is like _____ because
both _____."

MAPPING
Think of an upcoming opportunity to use the new idea in classes.
"_____, I'm gonna use _____
when _____."

INNOVATING
Think of an application for a "real life" setting.
"Outside of school, I could use _____
when _____."

Transfer Strategy #4:
MODEL EXAMPLES of how the skill or strategy has been used by showing or referring to explicit models.

Transfer Strategy #5:
CREATE CONNECTIONS by promoting risk-taking that stretches learning across content and into life.

ANALYSIS FOR BIAS

☒ Critical Thinking   ☐ Creative Thinking

PROGRAM: Skill: Analysis For Bias   **PASSWORD:** Acronym: BIAS

DATA BASE: Definition: Examining material for point-of-view and possible misrepresentation.

LIST: Synonyms: prejudiced, bigoted, slanted

SCAN: Examples: Advertising

ENTER: *When to use:*

> Reading, listening and acting as a critical thinker with advertising, political speaker, articles, etc.

MENU: *How to use:*

> **B**e aware of point-of-view
> **I**ndicate spottings of bias clues (EOIOC):
>
> > **E**xaggeration
> > **O**vergeneralization
> > **I**mbalance
> > **O**pinion as fact
> > **C**harged words
>
> **A**ccount for possible bias by citing proofs
> **S**tate opinion based on 'reasoned judgment'

DEBUGGING: *What to do if:*

> > —not sure of point-of-view; go on; try to discover.
> > —cannot find bias clues explicitly; articulate *feeling*, then pinpoint *why* you feel that way, re-examine data.

VISUAL LAYOUT: Patterns: Thought Tree
                                          Venn Diagram

FILE: Sample Lesson: History

                       History: Presidential Profile

(Analysis for bias: charged words.) Distribute both copies of the piece to opposite sides of the room. Have students analyze the attributes of the president on a web. Then ask them to *tell* what kind of man they think he was. Using the webs, analyze for bias.

The President achieved notoriety by stubbornly, bitterly, fanatically asserting his impudent pretensions even in legislative councils, through his tools who cunningly situated themselves on those councils. The Senate being in accord with his prejudices succumbed to his domination. He was a man of superstition and of obstinancy whose policy combined bigotry and arrogance with cowardice.

He was a creature of strong biases and belonged in the camp of the reactionaries. His conduct of the presidency portended a degeneration of that office into one of dictatorship.

The President achieved fame by firmly, steadfastly and gallantly presenting his insightful plans even in legislative councils through his colleagues who honorably seated themselves into those councils. The Senate, being in accord with his views, supported his leadership. He was a man of foresight and of integrity whose policy combined justice and confidence with courage.

He was a man of conviction and belonged in the league of visionaries. His portrayal of the presidency projected an elevation of that office into one of dignity.

Focus: Distribute the two versions to groups of students on opposite sides of the room without revealing differences. Have them do an attribute web from the readings. Post webs and discuss different profiles and possible points of view represented.

Be aware of point-of-view from title, source, etc.
Indicate bias clues: EOIOC
Account for possible bias (i.e. charged words)
State opinion based on 'reasoned judgment'

INDEX: Suggested Applications:

LANGUAGE ARTS: ● Journalism
                    ● Characters in a Novel

MATH: ● Graphs (Possible distortions)
                    ● Perspectives
                    ● Optical Illusions
                    ● Statistics

SCIENCE: ● Off-shore Oil Drilling
                    ● Environmental Issues
                    ● Evolution vs. Creation

SOCIAL STUDIES: ● Current Events: Summit Meeting
                      (Russia/USA)
                    ● Civil War (South/North)
                    ● Industrial Park
                    ● Community Issues
                    ● Super Highway

STRATEGIES

CATCH THEM
READY TO THINK

THE LISTENING POST

| **BACKGROUND** | To make it easy for students to share thinking, it helps if they develop listening and speaking skills. As we listen to each other, |

our bodies and behaviors tell the person speaking more than we realize. By sensitizing students to helpful and non-helpful listening behaviors, we lay the groundwork for more productive classroom discussions.

THINKING SKILL: ACTIVE LISTENING

| **FOCUS ACTIVITY** | Divide students into pairs. Designate the taller student in each pair as B; the other is A. Have all B's attend to the first instructions: |

1. Think of a time in your life when you had something important to tell your friends, but no one would listen. Prepare to describe that event to your partner. What did you want to say? Who didn't listen? What happened?

2. B's recall the story while the A's are given their instructions.

3. A's will recall what it takes to be a good listener. [i.e. you look at the person (eye contact), you nod your head, you look interested, you lean slightly forward, you don't interrupt, you smile.] Good listening takes hard work.

| **OBJECTIVE** | To identify helpful listening behaviors. |

| **INPUT** | On the overhead or board list behaviors. Ask the students to tell you what they see or note when someone is listening to them. Demonstrate or provide the clues they need. |

| **ACTIVITY** | Instructions: |

1. Check that the story tellers are ready.

2. Check that the others have an idea of what behavior is expected of a good listener. After they assent, tell them that they are to work with the assigned partner, but they may *not listen* to the partner. They are to behave the opposite of how a good listener behaves as long as they follow these simple rules: (1) stay in room; and (2) nobody gets hurt.

3. Encourage the story tellers to follow the same rules and try to get their story told.

4. After two minutes, signal the students to stop, return to their seats and attend to you.

5. Instruct the non-listeners to apologize and shake hands for their misbehavior.

6. Ask the story tellers to describe the non-listening behaviors they experienced. Make a master list.

METACOGNITIVE DISCUSSION

1. Change the pairs. Invite students to pick a different partner. Give instructions to the new pairs.

   A. Study the non-helpful behaviors. Make a joint list of the opposite behaviors which would tell you that someone *was* listening to you. (3 minutes)

   B. Take your partner and make a foursome with another pair.

   C. Share your lists and find the helpful behavior you all agree upon. Make a master list of the agreed upon items. (6 minutes)

2. On the board construct an unduplicated list from the sub-groups. Ask a variety of students to select the item that is most important . Each will explain his/her selection. Encourage all to practice the items as they listen to each speaker.

3. Discuss the value of helpful listening behaviors in classroom discussions.

CLOSURE

In the LOG, invite students to list the helpful listening behaviors they do best, the helpful behaviors they might work to improve, and at least one situation in which they might practice the helpful listening.

OR

Ask students to vote on a classroom code of conduct built on the helpful listening behaviors. Each item from the master list that receives a unanimous vote will be in the code. Ask for volunteers to prepare a code card to hang or duplicate the code for each individual's LOG.

PACTS

BACKGROUND

The positive climate necessary for skillful thinking is included with skillful communication. The five basic communication pre-skills encourage the positive interaction which marks the clear interchange of ideas.

PRE-SKILLS

Paraphrasing, affirming, clarifying, testing options and sensing.

FOCUS ACTIVITY

Write the word "compact" on the overhead or board. Follow with the synonyms contract, agreement, charter, or PACTS. Explain the definition of "compact" as a formal agreement between 2 people or an agreement or pact to **com**municate with others. Share examples from history such as the "MayFlower Compact." Ask several students to explain the word "compact" with their own examples. Conclude by highlighting on the overhead or board how the word PACTS & Com = Communication Pacts.

OBJECTIVE

To identify 5 communication skills which make a contract between listener and speaker for 2-way communication.

INPUT

On the board or overhead display the word:

P
A
C
T
S

Note to the students that the word is a tool which will help them remember 5 key skills which will help them communicate more successfully. Fill in each letter, define the skill and demonstrate with an example. Encourage the students to write their menu in their LOGS.

P = Paraphrase or play back. Ask a student to read this. "In a paraphrase, I repeat the key ideas stated to me. I don't add my own ideas or change the ideas to say what I want. I am like a recorder that plays back what it has recorded." Demonstrate paraphrasing by labeling what you are going to do and then paraphrase the above statement. Conclude by asking several different students to paraphrase a short statememt that you have selected from today's newspaper.

A = Affirming or appreciating. Ask a student to read this statement. "Affirming means that I tell a person I like what they are doing, saying or thinking." Label that you are going to affirm the student for reading the definition. " (NAME) , I liked how _(adverb)_ you read that statement." Conclude by asking several students to make an affirmative statement to another student. Affirm their efforts.

C = Clarify or check on specific details. Ask a student to read this statement, "Clarifying means to check what someone means by asking the person to describe in more detail, give an example, or be more specific about words we don't understand." Identify that you are going to model a clarifying question so that they have a specific example. "If I were to clarify or make more clear the word clarify, I would say "please give me an example of clarify." If I wanted you to clarify the word difficult, I might say, "describe a job you had to do which you thought was difficult." Then you might tell me about last night's homework. As a result, we would both be clearer in understanding what you meant. Conclude by asking a student to read this sentence. "Thinking is fun." Ask other students to ask clarifying questions.

T = Testing Options or trying out ideas. Ask a student to read this statement. "Testing options means to help the person I am talking with explore different possible answers." Identify that you are going to model this skill. Ask a student "What is one skill you have learned?" Affirm the answer and repeat the last question. Conclude by telling students that you are going to affirm helpful communication behaviors you have observed in the class. After you give each one, tell them that volunteers may use the "T" skill with you until you signal a stop. Start with "The first helpful skill I have observed being used is..."

S = Sensing or seeking out feelings. Ask a student to read the following. "Sensing or seeking out feelings means that I try to capture how a person is feeling about the idea. Is the person angry, sad, happy? When I sense a feeling I not only listen to the words but I listen to the tone of voice and watch the body language." Tell the class that the reader will repeat the description and that you will ask them to paraphrase the statement. After the second reading and several paraphrases, invite students to ask clarifying questions about "S." You will also want them to practice the "T" by asking you to demonstrate different emotional tones and non-verbal behaviors so that they can "sense" the tone.

Conclude with a summary review and check for understanding.

ACTIVITY | Instructions:

1. Divide the class into groups of *three*. If there is one four, divide it into two pairs. In each trio, have students label themselves as Piff, Poof & Pop.

2. Indicate that each of the following tasks will rotate at your signal. Display the tasks on the overhead, or give each trio a worksheet as well as the check chart.

   A. Observer (Start with POP): listens to the dialogue but focuses on the listener. Each time the listener uses a PACTS skill, the observer will check the chart.

   B. Listener (Start with POOF): listens to the speaker and practices PACTS as appropriate.

   C. Speaker (Start with PIFF): Talks for 1 - 2 minutes on one of the listed topics and then responds to the listener.

   (1) My dream vacation... (4) My favorite sport...
   (2) A hero I admire... (5) The food I hate the most...
   (3) A place I'd love to travel... (6) A topic of my choice...

D. Check that all understand the task by asking different students to paraphrase the instructions for each role.

3. Review the check chart.

NAME		P	A	C	T	S
PIFF	_____					
POOF	_____					
POP	_____					

4. Each five minutes, rotate the jobs. Affirm positive behaviors at the end of each round.

METACOGNITIVE DISCUSSION Encourage the students to continue the PACTS practice through this discussion. Ask the following questions. Extend responses with modeling of PACTS.

1. When someone is talking with you and paraphrases your ideas, what happens with your own thinking? What other reactions do you have?

2. When someone asks you to clarify, what happens with your thinking? What other reactions do you have?

3. What are the benefits to your thinking when you use PACTS in your communication?

4. How might a PACTS skill hinder your thinking?

CLOSURE In your LOG, list some situations in which you could improve your communication by using PACTS.

OR

In your LOG, pick one situation in which an historic or literary character you know might have benefited by using PACTS. Explain your choice.

OR

With a partner, select the PACTS skill which you want to continue practicing and explain how it will help your communication in a specific situation. Let each be on focus for three minutes and practice as you listen.

NOTE: With less mature students, you may want to break this lesson into smaller units, shorter time and more guided practice. For each PACTS skill, you may select age-appropriate vocabulary, short recordings, video tape news items, or daily editorials. Encourage all students to use these skills as you give corrective and affirmative feedback.

NOTES

STEMS

BACKGROUND Helping students focus on what they are learning is a difficult task. Motivating students to write about how they are thinking about thinking (metacognition) is even more difficult. One simple tool is the *stem* or *lead-in*. Like the stem that connects the leaf to the limb of a bush or tree, the stem statement connects a student's thinking to the content taught in your course. From the stem grows ideas for writing, discussing and sharing.

THINKING SKILL: REFLECTING

FOCUS ACTIVITY On the board or overhead, write the word "stem." Conduct an all class discussion (no right answers, seek many responses to each question, clarify answers) with these questions:

1. What does the word "stem" mean to you?

2. Give examples of "stems" you have seen in nature or real life. Explain the purpose of each.

OBJECTIVE To use stems as a tool for thinking about thinking.

INPUT Explain that a "stem" is an extension and summarize examples (glass stem, leaf stem, etc.). Where appropriate, use visuals to show stems.

ACTIVITY Instructions:

1. Inform the students that they are going to use stems as a lead-in for writing tasks. These stems will help them get started on writing about ideas that they are studying in class.

2. On the overhead, show a list of possible stems...

   I think...   I believe...   I discovered...   I wonder...

3. Point out the first person pronoun "I" and the thinking or learning verb. Add others to the list from student ideas.

4. Show how you will use the stems in a *context*. The context is the discussion topic for the day. For instance, if the class were discussing "courage," the context would begin: "*Today about courage*, I discovered..."

5. Check for understanding by asking volunteers to explain "stems" in their own words and to give *new* examples.

6. Divide the class into groups of three. Give each group a copy of an editorial from the newspaper. Assign one student in each group to read the editorial to the others in that group.

7. Instruct the group to brainstorm a list of stems which apply to the editorial (i.e. "From this editorial, I learned...").

8. Exchange lists among groups. Each member will select one stem from the new list and complete it for their own editorial.

METACOGNITIVE DISCUSSION

1. What stem did you select?

2. How did the stem help you to think about the editorial?

3. How else might you use a stem in your school work?

4. How might you improve your thinking by using stems at the end of each school day?

CLOSURE   Instruct the students to select one of the following stems:

> About stems, I learned...
> About stems, I think...
> About stems, I plan...
> About stems, I wonder...

Ask each student to share their completed stem.

ONE POTATO, TWO POTATO

BACKGROUND Keen observation is a prerequisite for skillful thinking. Students can learn to be sharper observers with all their senses. For this activity, you will need one potato per student and a large box.

THINKING SKILL: OBSERVING

FOCUS ACTIVITY Review with the students what their five senses are and why each sense is important. Ask them what life might be like for a person who is missing one of the senses.

OBJECTIVE To sharpen our ability to observe with our senses.

INPUT Make a list of the 5 senses. Provide or brainstorm a list of adjectives which an observer might use to describe a sensation (i.e. touch: smooth, rough). Conclude with a list of reasons why it is so important to our thinking that we observe carefully.

ACTIVITY Instructions:

1. Arrange the students to sit in a giant circle. Tell them that you are going to pass a box around the circle. Each is to take out one potato and study it with all their senses. It will be very important for them to study carefully since they will soon have a test of how well they have observed all the special details which make their potato different from all other potatoes.

2. Allow the students several minutes to study their potatoes. They must observe carefully.

3. After several minutes of observing, check to see if they could, when asked, pick out their potato from all the rest even if blindfolded. Pass the box around the circle and collect the potatoes.

4. Instruct the students to close their eyes and keep them closed as you pass out potatoes. Hand the first potato from the box and pass it to your right. Tell each student to test out the potato. If anyone finds his/her potato, he/she should keep it without saying anything or opening the eyes. If not, pass the potato on.

5. Slowly hand all potatoes to the right. If any come back to you, send them around the circle again. When all have claimed a potato, tell the students to open their eyes and check their potato.

ONE POTATO, TWO POTATO

METACOGNITIVE DISCUSSION
Ask the students to comment on these questions:

1. How did you know that you had *your* potato? What were the clues you used?

2. If you were to do this task over, what would you do differently?

3. What did you learn about observing?

CLOSURE
In your LOG, complete one of these tasks:

1. Imagine that a creature from another planet was observing you. List the unique characteristics he would report about you.

2. Imagine that you are a news reporter who must describe your best friend in a news story. What are the special characteristics you would report?

3. Pretend that you are giving directions to a relative about how to find your house. What are the unique characteristics which will make your house or apartment building stand out from all the others on the street?

THE PEOPLE SEARCH

BACKGROUND In Bloom's Taxonomy, comprehension or understanding is the second level of cognition. In that category, explaining is one subset. When students can explain an idea in their own words, we have a signal that basic understanding is at least starting.

THINKING SKILL: UNDERSTANDING

FOCUS ACTIVITY Show the students a picture of snow. Ask several students to explain what "snow" is as if speaking to a person who cannot see. Paraphrase each answer.

OBJECTIVE To express a clear understanding of a concept.

INPUT Explain to the students how important it is to express a clear understanding of ideas. Explanations are not memorized statements, but translations. In a translation, we put concepts or ideas into our own words, give examples and describe. For instance, a radio newscaster must explain how a snow storm paralyzed a city. She must use her own words or read the words of a writer so that she gives a clear picture of the evidence. Policemen must explain broken laws. Teachers explain school rules. Parents explain why children cannot play in the street.

ACTIVITY Instructions:

1. Distribute a copy of "people search" to each student. Review the instructions on the sheet. Check for clarity of instructions before starting the 10 minute search. (You may wish to change the key words in the six blocks. Use concepts from a topic you are studying or from a unit you are ready to start. In any case, be sure the words you use are age and experience appropriate to your students.)

2. After 10 minutes, instruct all to sit down.

THE PEOPLE SEARCH

METACOGNITIVE DISCUSSION

1. Instruct the students to raise their hands for each "yes."

    A. You finished all six blocks.

    B. You can explain in your own words each item.

    C. You have an item you don't quite understand.

2. Ask volunteers to explain each block. Begin with those identified in (c) above. When a student is unsure, make sure he/she listens to the students' explanations and then gives one of his/her own.

3. Ask students to make clear to the class why "explaining" is important

4. Ask students to tell the class what they experience happening with their own thinking when they are asked to explain an idea.

| CLOSURE | Assign students to pair up with a nearby student . On the overhead or board show a plus-minus chart. Give each pair 5 minutes to list as many reasons why (**a**) explaining is helpful to thinking (+); and (**b**) it is not helpful (—). After 5 minutes ask students to explain their answers. Build a master list on the overhead or board. Conclude by returning to the objective and highlighting the objective.

PEOPLE SEARCH

Find someone who:

Can classify friends into four groups. _____	**Reads the newspaper (or parts of it) daily** _____
Likes mysteries and can often predict the outcomes. _____	**Can list 5 steps she/he uses in solving a problem.** _____
Is a "computer addict." _____	**Can brainstorm ten "m" words in one minute.** _____

THE THINKER'S PENCIL bookmark...

PATTERNS FOR THINKING

EVALUATION
- Decide
- Rank
- Defend
- Verify
- Critique

SYNTHESIS
- Hypothesize
- Infer
- Predict
- Imagine
- Estimate
- Invent

ANALYSIS
- Compare/Contrast
- Make an analogy
- Classify
- Sequence
- Give cause

APPLICATION
- Apply
- Demonstrate
- Illustrate
- Generalize
- Show how

ILLINOIS RENEWAL INSTITUTE, INC.

PATTERNS FOR THINKING

EVALUATION
- Decide
- Rank
- Defend
- Verify
- Critique

SYNTHESIS
- Hypothesize
- Infer
- Predict
- Imagine
- Estimate
- Invent

ANALYSIS
- Compare/Contrast
- Make an analogy
- Classify
- Sequence
- Give cause

APPLICATION
- Apply
- Demonstrate
- Illustrate
- Generalize
- Show how

ILLINOIS RENEWAL INSTITUTE, INC.

ASK THE RIGHT QUESTION

BACKGROUND In the marketing field, a basic operating principle is "ask the right question and you will get the answers you need. Ask the wrong question and you will get chaos." To learn how to ask the right question, the one that will give the answer we want, is a difficult skill to master. When asking the question in the context of skillful thinking, what we want is responses that show the students are applying thinking skills well. This means the students recognize what type or level of thinking is being asked (Critical or Creative? Analytical? Evaluative?) and how to use the needed mental operations.

To help students recognize what they are being asked to do as thinkers and to facilitate using different thinking skills, it helps that they learn labels, definitions and samples as "mental coat hooks" on which to hang their thinking patterns. One highly successful method is to teach the students patterns of questions. Although it is not the only approach, nor was it compiled for this purpose, Bloom's cognitive taxonomy serves as a useful tool.

THINKING SKILL: INVESTIGATING

FOCUS ACTIVITY On the overhead, display this saying:

"Even if you are on the right track, you will get run over if you just sit there." Will Rogers

Ask the following questions. Allow wait-time. Seek multiple responses to each question. In the last question, encourage students to supply a rationale or proof of the judgements. Don't forget DOVE.

1. In your own words, explain the key idea of the quote.

2. What would result if you were to use this idea with your school work?

3. What assumptions does Rogers make about life?

4. Propose your own theory about life.

5. Agree or disagree with Rogers. Give proof for your answer.

OBJECTIVE To identify four (4) patterns for asking questions.

INPUT Give each student a copy of The Thinker Pencil.

They can include the page in their notes or cut out the pencil for a bookmark. You may also want to make a larger poster copy of the pencil and keep it displayed in the front of the room. Discuss the importance of asking the right question and the value of thinking about information in a variety of ways. Questions not only seek answers, but if open ended, they will stimulate thinking.

When you give out the pencils, spend some time reviewing the vocabulary or assign students to use the dictionary. Check for understanding.

ASK THE RIGHT QUESTION

ACTIVITY | Instructions:

1. Select a story, paragraph from student text, popular song, a short video documentary, news editorial, a non-fiction article from a magazine, etc., and give a copy to each student.

2. Assign the students to groups of three. Give each group a sheet of newsprint, tape and markers. Select recorder, leader and time keeper.

3. Allow 15 minutes for the task. Each group will invent 4 questions, one from each group on the pencil about the story or article. (You may want each group to use a different article.) The recorder will write the question on the newsprint.

4. Post the questions and instruct each group leader to walk through the questions, labeling the type of question being asked (i.e. analysis, synthesis, etc.) Give feedback and modify.

METACOGNITIVE DISCUSSION | Ask the following questions. Seek multiple responses.

1. Explain in your own words and give an example of the following: application, analysis, synthesis, evaluation.

2. Explain how you might use each of the different levels of questions if you were a teacher.

3. What are some sound reasons for learning the different ways to think?

4. What would happen to you if you had to answer analytic and evaluative questions in every class?

CLOSURE | In your LOG, write an editorial in which you defend the current way grades are given in your school (or some other practice of student interest).

THE STRAW PUZZLE

BACKGROUND When faced with problems, skilled problem-solvers are patient, reflective and willing to try new approaches. Poor problem solvers rush in where angels fear to tread, act impulsively, and quit quickly. By learning how to approach problem-solving with care and investigation, each of us can increase our problem-solving capabilities.

THINKING SKILL: EXPLORING POINTS OF VIEW

FOCUS ACTIVITY On the overhead or board, place 9 dots as follows:

•   •   •

•   •   •

•   •   •

Tell the students that they have 5 minutes, working together or alone to connect all 9 dots with 4 straight lines. Once they have placed the pencil on the paper they may not lift it off.

After 5 minutes, allow volunteers to present their solutions. If there are none, show them this solution.

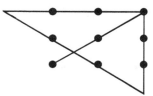

1. Ask: "How is this solution different from your solution? What did you have to think about differently to solve the puzzle?" (looking from a different point of view; exploring different ways.)

2. Ask the students who were unsuccessful to describe how they were thinking as they worked with the lines. On the overhead list key words. Ask them to mark a "+" with the steps that helped them and a "−" with the steps that didn't help. Note how exploration, trying new and different patterns was important.

OBJECTIVE To encourage students to explore multiple points-of-view when solving problems.

INPUT Highlight exploration by pointing out how a different point of view was critical to breaking out of the narrow boundaries first seen. Conclude by tracing how you might think through the line problem. Highlight these procedures:

THE STRAW PUZZLE

a. Take time to review the task.

b. Explore your visual memory to review different geometric forms (i.e. squares, triangles, etc.) in different patterns (buildings, furniture, etc.).

c. Seek several different arrangements.

d. Try different points of view.

ACTIVITY

1. Divide the students into pairs. Give each pair six (6) equal length straws.

2. Instruct one partner to use the six straws to make 4 triangles. The "builder" will follow TEST, thinking out loud.

3. The observer will write down the out loud thinking.

4. If there are no successful pyramids (3-D Model) after 5 minutes, reverse the roles. As soon as there are at least 2 successful builders, stop. If there are none after the second 5 minutes, stop and demonstrate the solution.

METACOGNITIVE DISCUSSION

1. Ask several different unsuccessful builders to describe their thinking as they used TEST to build the triangles. Paraphrase the key elements and list on the board.

2. Repeat the descriptions with the successful builders. List the key elements.

3. Ask students to identify the similar view in the two lists. Give emphasis to "exploring points of view."

4. Ask students to identify the differences. Invite students to clarify with specifics.

5. Ask students to identify how they might approach a similar visual problem differently. Paraphrase responses and solicit specific examples.

CLOSURE
In the thinking LOG, ask students to complete one of these stems:

About "exploring points of view" in problem solving,

> I learned...
> I discovered...
> I wonder...
> I intend...

If time allows, invite volunteers to share.

MRS. POTTER

BACKGROUND A critical thinker is often described as a person who can evaluate the quality of thinking used to solve problems. The critical thinker makes sound, logical judgments about ideas, he/she studies, reads, sees on TV or in the movies, and hears from friends, politicians, neighbors or peers. The thinking skills required for solid evaluation, however, are very difficult and complex. Before a student masters the complexities of evaluation, it is important that they develop a positive atttitude about evaluation as a learning tool.

THINKING SKILL: EVALUATING

FOCUS ACTIVITY Project Mrs. Potter's Questions on the overhead or hand a copy of the sheet to each student. Review the questions with the students in preparation for the task.

1. What were you expected to do?

2. In this assignment, what did you do well?

3. If you had to do this task over, what would you do differently?

4. What help do you need from me?

OBJECTIVE To identify four basic self-evaluation questions, which will help you in judging the quality of your work and your thinking.

INPUT Indicate to the students that the word "evaluate" means to weigh, to judge or to determine the value of something. One important evaluator is oneself. As we learn to evaluate, we set standards by which we judge the quality of our thinking and our work.

ACTIVITY Instructions:

A. Remind the students that after each group completes the task, the group will list responses to each of Mrs. Potter's Questions. Give each group a worksheet with the 4 questions.

B. Assign three students to each group.

C. Give each group a copy of these task instructions and review them.

HOW IS...?

1. Assign an official group recorder. All will keep ideas and notes in their own *LOGS*, but the official recorder will turn in the worksheets.

2. Follow the DOVE Guidelines.

3. For each question, make a list of answers. You will have 10 minutes to get *as many* answers as possible for your group for the questions listed. Be sure you have at least 2 answers to each question.

    a. How is a TV like a snowflake?
    b. How is a table like a glove?
    c. How is a bird like a lightbulb?
    d. How is a house like a flower?
    e. How is a book like a shoe?

D.   At the end of ten minutes, end the task.

E.   Instruct each group to take 10 minutes to respond to Mrs. Potter's questions *as a group*. They may list items about the *group* or about *individuals* in the group. Instruct them to be specific especially looking at how well they followed the given instructions, (i.e. DOVE, time, balance of questions) as well as the quality of the answers given. The recorder will write out the group responses for class sharing and to submit to you.

F.   Sample responses to each question with the entire class.

METACOGNITIVE DISCUSSION

1. What are Mrs. Potter's four questions? (Write on board or overhead)

2. Put the four questions into your own words. (Select a variety of different answers for each)

3. In your schoolwork, what/when would it help you to ask yourself these four questions? (List the various responses)

4. What would be different about your homework (or substitute another opportunity) if you used Mrs. Potter's questions to evaluate how you did?

CLOSURE   Assign the students to use Mrs. Potter's questions with a homework assignment. Instruct them to hand in a Mrs. Potter's worksheet with the asssignment.

MRS. POTTER'S QUESTIONS

1. **What were you expected to do?**

2. **In this assignment, what did you do well?**

3. **If you had to do this task over, what would you do differently?**

4. **What help do you need from me?**

NOTES

CATCH THEM
THINKING CRITICALLY

THE ATTRIBUTE WEB

BACKGROUND No thinking skill is more basic to critical thinking than attribute determination. Being able to determine those essential characteristics of a person, place, thing or idea that make it similar or different to others, helps us define and classify objects. Without this skill students mix up ideas, become confused and have no way to sort out or group objects.

THINKING SKILL: ATTRIBUTING

FOCUS ACTIVITY Invite three students who have three similar characteristics (i.e. hair or eye color, shoes, height) to stand in the front of the class.) Ask the remaining students to tell why you selected this group.

OBJECTIVE To identify critical attributes by which one can group or classify like objects.

INPUT On the overhead, write the words:

> **5 S** = **S**ense
> **S**ound
> **S**mell
> **S**ize
> **S**pecialty

Using a cow, a flower and a bar of soap, show how we use sense (taste and touch), sound (noise and voice), smell (odor), size (height, weight, width, depth) and specialty (use) to define or describe an object via our 5 senses (smell, taste, touch, hearing, sight). The information we gather through our senses gives us the characteristics of objects. The unique arrangement of characteristics allows us to determine what an object is. When we group or classify all objects with similar characteristics, this unique arrangement of traits allows us to be more accurate. Those unique characteristics which are true only of a special group are called critical attributes.

On the board or overhead, draw this demonstration attribute web.

Ask the students to give you characteristics or attributes which will describe a sneaker. Put up all ideas given on the rays. After you have filled 10 to 20 rays, ask the class to identify only those characteristics which are true of all sneakers. Star (*) those and indicate that these are the critical attributes.

THE ATTRIBUTE WEB

ACTIVITY

Instructions:

1. Put 5 - 7 students in a huddle. Instruct each student to select 3 other students with at least one characteristic (non-critical attributes) in common with themselves and sit down in a group of four.

2. Assign by height a leader, a timekeeper, a recorder, materials manager and an observer in each group.

3. Have the recorder pick up newsprint, marker and tape for the group.

4. Prepare timekeeper for a 10 minute task. Observers will have to note what each person did to help in addition to his/her special job.

5. Instruct the recorder to draw a large attribute web on the newsprint. From a hat or box, have each leader pick out one of these titles or others of your choice to place in the center of the web:

   - paragraph
   - peace
   - family
   - light bulb
   - addition
   - dentist

6. With each person contributing in turn or saying, "I pass," allow 10 minutes for web work.

7. At the end of the time, instruct the group to select the critical attributes from its web. Post and discuss the webs.

METACOGNITIVE DISCUSSION

1. Ask several groups to identfify the critical attributes selected. Ask them to describe how they made the selection decision.

2. How did the 5 "**S**'s" help them select the critical attributes?

3. How might the web help them in social studies? English or reading? math? science? Ask individuals to describe a specific example in each academic area.

4. What did each member add to the discussion? Give examples.

CLOSURE

In the LOGS, instruct students to respond to the following:

1. In your own words, explain the term "critical attribute."

2. Make a web for a reading assignment in _____. Identify the critical attributes of the material read. (You may wish to discuss these in class the next day.)

THE VENN DIAGRAM

THINKING SKILL: COMPARE & CONTRAST

FOCUS ACTIVITY
Review with students the word "attribute." Provide other synonyms and ask students to explain the 5 "**S**'s" *(sense, sound, smell, size and specialty).*

Show them two similar objects in the classroom and ask them to list in their LOGS how the objects are similar or alike (i.e. Your teacher's desk and a student's desk). Ask for samples to write on the overhead or board. Next, ask students to list characteristics which are not alike or not similar in the objects. Again, list samples on the board or overhead.

OBJECTIVE
To use the Venn Diagram as a tool for comparing and contrasting like objects.

INPUT
Explain how we compare items by showing how they are alike or similar and that we contrast by showing how the items are different. Discuss how the 5 "**S**'s" can help us compare and contrast not only the obvious characteristics, but also the more subtle critical attributes. Give synonyms for "obvious" and "subtle" and provide examples of obvious and subtle distinctions.

Finally, indicate that you are going to show them how to use a visual format, the Venn Diagram, to help in the identification of similar and different characteristics. Demonstrate on the board or overhead with this model.

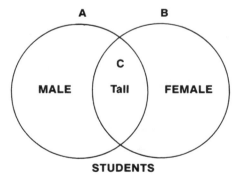

1. Call two students to the front of the class.

2. Invite the class to list the unique features of each in A & B. In C, they will list characteristics common to both.

3. Point out that A & B contain the differences which they can contrast. C contains the similar items for comparing.

THE VENN DIAGRAM

ACTIVITY | Instructions:

1. Divide the class into new groups of three. Give each group a sheet of newsprint, a marker and tape. Assign a recorder, materials manager, a leader and a timekeeper/observer.

2. Give each trio two similar objects. (i.e. an apple and orange, a pencil and marker, a book and a videotape, etc.) Instruct the trio to do a careful analysis in 10 minutes of the similarities and differences by using the Venn Diagram.

3. After 10 minutes, post the results.

METACOGNITIVE DISCUSSION

1. Review the diagrams by asking each leader to highlight the subtle and/or obvious similarities and/or differences. (Vary the task for each chart.)

2. Ask individuals to retrace how they approached the task. Use paraphrasing and clarifying responses.

3. Ask students what different "thinking styles" or ways of thinking about the task they noticed in their trio? In the class?

4. Ask observers to comment on what similar characteristics they noted in the "Thinking Styles" within their trio as they worked on the task. Note that there are no single, "right" answers to this question. Clarify and paraphrase as needed.

5. Construct on the board or overhead a Venn Diagram which illustrates the similarities and differences of "Thinking Styles" used to complete this task.

CLOSURE | Ask for several "application to school work" examples for instances in which use of the Venn Diagram would be a helpful study tool. (i.e. In writing a comparison essay in Literature class.)

Instruct students to make new groups of three. Each group will select one new way to use the Venn Diagram as a learning aid. They will prepare instructions for completing the Venn Diagram on the learning task they selected. Using newsprint, they will display and review the product with the class.

WHAT'S YOUR RATING?

BACKGROUND "Performance Standards" are an important part of evaluation. On the job, employees are rated against performance standards. Test cars are measured against performance standards. All around us, standards measure degrees of success.

THINKING SKILL: COMPARING AGAINST A STANDARD

FOCUS ACTIVITY On the overhead or board, show a rating scale:

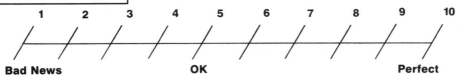

Remind the students of the "perfect 10" scale they have all heard about. Invite three students to the front of the class. Indicate a mock "10" scale across the front of the room. Ask the students to rate themslves as you give the standards.

(A) 1 = My room is a daily disaster. "Daily Disaster Dan"

10 = Neat as a pin always. "Ned Neat"

(B) 1 = Never prepared for any class. "Fran Fake It"

10 = Always ready. "Rachel Ready"

(C) 1 = A junk food diet. "Junking Jim"

10 = Healthy food only. "Healthy Hank"

OBJECTIVE To identify ways to rate their performance in accordance with standards.

INPUT On the board or overhead, draw and explain several common ways to measure performance.

A. THE RATING SCALE

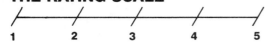

B. THE WEIGHT SCALE

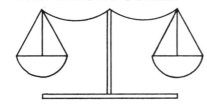

C. THE LINE GRAPH

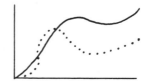

D. THE METER

With the class, brainstorm possible advantages and uses of each.

WHAT'S YOUR RATING?

1. Divide the class into pairs. Instruct each pair to select a scale or graph from those provided or to make one of their own. Give each pair 2 sheets of 8 ½ X 11″ paper, a marker and tape.

2. Instruct the pair to select a "performance" from the list and match it up with the scale selected. Avoid duplicate topics. Make 2 copies of the scale.

> a. Promptness to Class
> b. Kindness
> c. Hard Work
> d. Study Habits
> e. Helpfulness
> f. Cheerfulness
> g. Energy
> h. Creativity
> i. Neatness
> j. Cooperation
> k. Sincerity
> l. Honesty
> m. Willingness to Share
> n. Follow Through
> o. Trustworthiness
> p. _____
> q. _____
> r. _____

3. Each will take his/her copy of the scale and seek signatures from other students. No student should sign any pair's sheet more than once. Each should put his/her own initials on the scale nearest where he/she is. Allow a 5 minute mingle.

METACOGNITIVE DISCUSSION

1. What did you discover about setting a standard?

2. What type of thinking did this task require? In making the scale? In signing?

3. What would help you make a more accurate rating for yourself on the scale?

CLOSURE | In your LOG, design a rating scale and mark your performance in completing both aspects of this task.

CLUES

BACKGROUND Drawing inferences is much like filling in a missing clue. Students must discover the hidden, or at least, less obvious connections between words, phrases and sentences, and draw conclusions that are valid. Readers become like detectives as they search for the missing clues.

THINKING SKILL: CLASSIFYING

FOCUS ACTIVITY Ask students to identify the names of several detectives they know from reading, TV or movies. Ask what a detectve might conclude from these words: knife, blood, corpse. Indicate that the detective fills in the missing blanks by clustering words and drawing inferences.

OBJECTIVE To cluster or classify common words in order to draw inferences from limited data.

INPUT On overhead or handout introduce the acronym CLUES and explain what each letter represents.

C = Cluster like words

L = Label clusters

U = Untangle sub-clusters

E = Examine clusters and subclusters

S = SET Patterns

Explain how they can use the word CLUES to remind them how to group or *classify* words or concepts in order to identify the *inferences* suggested. Highlight the importance of *inferential* reading and show how it is much like the *clue* finding that detectives do.

Use the following collection of words to demonstrate how to use each letter in the acronym, CLUES. Go letter by letter and check for understanding. (radar, jet, flames, base, news, cost, fog)

Example:

C ▶ *Cluster* .... **1.** (radar, radio, TV, news) - **2.** (cloud, fog) - **3.** (airport, base, jet) - **4.** (flames, cost)
L ▶ *Label* .... **communications** (radio, radar, TV, news), **weather** (cloud, fog),
 planes (airport, jet, base), **accident** (flames, cost)
U ▶ *Untangle* ... **warning device:** (radar), **news announcement** (TV, news, radio)
E ▶ *Examine* ...

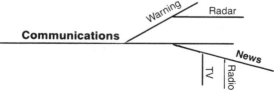

S ▶ *Set Pattern*..bad weather ◊ jet plane crash ◊ news ◊ news ◊ cost

CLUES

ACTIVITY Instructions:
1. Ask students to explain CLUES in their own words.

2. Use the overhead or handout worksheets with the words listed below in the attribute web.

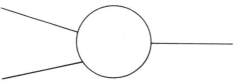

Students may work alone or in threes or twos. Provide newsprint or blank overheads for each group to work a web. They may add as many branches or sub-branches as they desire. The core concept will go in the middle. There is no one right answer, but groups will have to explain how and why they formed their clusters.

The words: astronaut, star seeker, laser beam, shuttle, booster rocket, gravity, lead boots, light years, solid fuel, capsule, heat shield, moon walker, launch pad.

(You may substitute any group of 20 - 40 words. Take an article from a newspaper or magazine or a chapter from the textbook. In your list include the title, sub-topic nouns, and a random selection of words from each sub-topic; mix the list.)

3. Allow 5 - 10 minutes for the completion of the webs.

4. Select one or more groups to explain their clusters. Encourage questions about "how" and "why" from the class about the sample webs. Be sure that the sample webs are visible (overhead or newsprint) to the class. Encourage acceptance of different classifications as long as the author group can explain its clusters.

METACOGNITIVE DISCUSSION

1. Review CLUES

2. Ask another sample group or two to trace the clustering they did with the webs in relation to the CLUES guidelines.

3. Identify which items students had difficulty in clustering. What did they do to solve the problem(s)?

4. What general rules can one make about "classifying" when clustering problems occur?

5. When might you use CLUES in your studies? When else might CLUES help your thinking?

CLOSURE In the thinking LOG have students:

A. Summarize CLUES in their own words.

B. Record "What to do if" guidelines for their future use.

C. List "good times to use" CLUES.

D. Practice with a new webbing from the class textbook or newspaper.

SCAVENGER HUNT

BACKGROUND

Classifying is one of the most basic thinking skills. From our earliest days, we learn to sort, to separate into groups, to make patterns based on similarities or differences. All around us we see samples of classifications: the yellow pages, greeting cards, aisles in the grocery store, zip codes, telephone exchanges, credit card numbers.

THINKING SKILL: CLASSIFYING

FOCUS ACTIVITY

Invite three students to come to the front of the classroom. (Pick three with very visible common characteristics such as eye glasses, the same color shirt, etc.) Ask the class to identify characteristics which all three have in common. (Watch out! They will find more than you intended, and that is OK!) After the class has identified some characteristics which allowed you to make the group, introduce the vocabulary: sort, group, characteristics and classify. "Classification is the thinking skill that helps us sort objects and ideas into groups according to their like characteristics."

OBJECTIVE

To examine the various helpful ways one can use the skill of classifying.

INPUT

Provide a mental menu for classification.

C = Cluster like words
L = Label clusters
U = Untangle sub-clusters
E = Examine clusters and subclusters
S = SET Patterns

ACTIVITY

Instructions:

1. Instruct students to form teams of three. The team members must have at least three visible characteristics which they all share in common.

2. On the Scavenger Hunt, each member, working alone, will have 5 minutes to gather no more than 5 items. Be sure that you determine the limits of the search area (i.e. in the classroom, in the school building, on school grounds, etc.), the time limits, and the untouchables (i.e. no objects from desks, must fit in the hand, etc.) Give some examples of possible objects that are OK to collect.

3. When the hunters return, instruct them to join their team and arrange their items in a small circle on the desk or floor.

4. Identify the roles: 1) the timekeeper will signal the end of each five minutes; 2) the recorder will write down the "outloud" thinking of the sorter as he/she completes the task; 3) the sorter will have five minutes to sort the team's objects into multiple groups (at least two objects to a group), identify the group's common characteristics (the more characteristics per group the merrier), and label the groups and subgroups. After each five minute sorting, rotate the

SCAVENGER HUNT

roles. The goal for each team: identify as many different ways to classify the assembled materials as possible.

5. After 15 minutes, call time. Instruct the teams: 1) to count the number of groups and subgroups identified and 2) to review the methods used to think through the task.

METACOGNITIVE DISCUSSION

1. Ask one team to report on the items it gathered and some of the groupings it made. Be sure the team explains why it made its groupings.

2. Select one or two more teams to give a similar report.

3. Ask a new team to report on one member's thinking approach to classification. On the board, record the description. Ask for clarification as needed.

4. Ask for another team to give a different description. Record this as well.

5. Gather a third report which marks any other differences in the thinking methods used. Record the differences.

6. Ask the students to raise their hands to signal which of the approaches was most like their own.

7. Ask several students to describe where else the skill of classifying might be helpful to them?

8. Name classification systems we use. (Dewey Decimal).

CLOSURE
In the thinking LOG, instruct students to record:

1. What do I do well as a classifier?
2. How can I improve my classifiying skills?
3. What questions do I have about classifying?

OPTIONAL CLOSURE
Use a wrap around with one of these stems:

A. About classifying, I learned...
B. About classifying, I wonder...
C. About classifying, I am pleased...

MILESTONES

THINKING SKILL: SEQUENCING

FOCUS ACTIVITY Select 10 students and invite them to stand in the front of the class. Instruct them to rearrange themselves by each of these instructions.

1. The tallest (far right) to the shortest (far left).

2. The oldest to the youngest.

3. The person who lives closest to the school to the person who lives farthest.

OBJECTIVE To use a milestone chart to sequence events.

INPUT Describe the milestone chart to students with a model on the board.

Just as they made a living chart, they are going to make a milestone chart to plan an event. Demonstrate with a major test.

A. List the tasks needed to prepare for the test (take notes in class, write down questions, view class notes, study reading notes, review notes, outline text assignment, take test , read text assignment, ask questions and discuss material.)

B. On the board, sequence the events by placing the event on the chart.

ACTIVITY Instructions:

1. Place students in groups of three. Provide each trio with a sheet of newsprint, marker and tape. Assign roles (recorder, reporter, checker). The recorder will draw the time line on the newsprint.

2. Instruct each two to list no more than 7 events which occur in *preparing* for one of the following:

A.   A big date
B.   Writing an essay
C.   Buying a car
D.   Winning the Super Bowl
E.   Taking a vacation
F.   Free choice topic

3.   After the group completes its list, instruct the group to sequence the events by time on the milestone chart.

METACOGNITIVE DISCUSSION

1.   Ask sample groups to describe their charts.

2.   Identify the procedures (list, order, chart) used to complete the chart.

3.   Ask how students might use the chart in their everyday lives. Have them specify their answers.

4.   What difficulties did they experience in making the chart? How did they handle the difficulties?

CLOSURE

Instruct the trios to prepare a milestone chart for a story from literature, a major current event or an historic incident they are studying. Post the charts.

THE PRIORITY LADDER

THINKING SKILL: SETTING PRIORITIES

FOCUS ACTIVITY Present the students with these *forced* choices. For each sample, they must select one or the other and explain *why*. For each sample, listen to several different responses/reasons. A choice and a reason are required even though many will protest "I can't."

1. Which do you prefer: peanut butter and jelly or ham and cheese?

2. Which do you like better: fruit or vegetables?

3. Which is more important for you: a good night's sleep or a good test grade?

OBJECTIVE To identify priorities needed to make choices or decisions.

INPUT Explain to the class that *priorities* are those values, beliefs, likes or interests that guide us in making selections or choices. A priority in selecting one food over another may be a health belief or a taste attraction. In some cases, both the "belief" and the "like" may be priorities which support each other. "I both like the apples and I believe they are more healthy." In other cases, they may conflict. "I know the apple is more healthy, but I hate the taste and want to spend my money on candy, which is less healthy." Which will come out as my #1 priority? The challenge comes when I must act on priorities. The more clearly I think through my beliefs, values, likes and interest and separate my priorities, the more easily I can evaluate situations in which I am challenged to make choices and decisions.

ACTIVITY Instructions:

1. On the board or overhead, sketch a priority ladder or give each student a pre-sketched worksheet.

THE PRIORITY LADDER

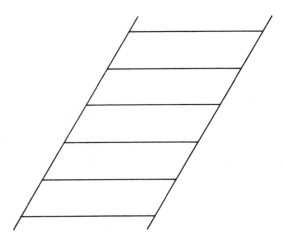

2. Project these words on the overhead: money, car, food, house, TV, job, friends.

3. Instruct each student to place the words on the ladder. In the *top* rung, place the word that is most important to you. Work down the ladder until you write in the least important in the bottom rung.

METACOGNITIVE DISCUSSION

1. Assign students to threes. Assign a rotation number (1,2,3). Number 1 will be our focus for 3 minutes. (You are the class timekeeper). In the three minutes, #1 will explain his/her ranks. The partners will follow DOVE as active listeners.

2. Rotate the focus persons each three minutes.

3. After all are completed, invite #2 from several different trios to report on the top priorities.

4. Discuss the important considerations one must make when setting a priority.

CLOSURE In the LOG, each student will take his/her top priority and sketch a 4-step ladder. On the ladder, the student will identify and rank the top benefits for the selected priority. (i.e. Car = (1) get to job; (2) emergencies; (3) family trips; and (4) going to store).

SHERLOCK HOLMES

| **BACKGROUND** | Detectives are great users of information bits. Not only do they observe carefully and search for the tiniest clues, they learn to use past experience as a way to help them organize the information they find. They exhibit some of the best qualities of the skillful thinker. They are persistent, precise, patient problem solvers. With the four P's, in this strategy, students will get a chance to act as detectives and find a missing character, one with characteristics beneficial to all of us.

To prepare the room you will have to plant the clues for students to find. Be sure that each clue has a mark to indicate that it is a clue so that someone won't accidently walk off with or move the clue.

THINKING SKILL: DRAWING CONCLUSIONS

| **FOCUS ACTIVITY** | Ask students to recall the names of the skilled detectives that they know from TV or reading. What are some of the characteristics that separate the skilled investigators from the unskilled? List the responses on the board, add your own and then highlight the 4 P's: Persistence, Precision, Patience and a Problem Solving Approach.

| **OBJECTIVE** | To draw valid conclusions from given facts.

| **ACTIVITY** | Instructions:

1. Match students in pairs. (A la Sherlock Holmes and Watson, Simon and Simon, Batman and Robin, etc.) Tell students that they are looking for twelve clues planted around the room and marked with a dot. They should observe each clue carefully and note down a full description.
   - (1) An assignment notebook
   - (2) A picture of a *student* at a desk. (Make this a young person. Without this clue, the answer can be a teacher)
   - (3) A bottle labeled "midnight oil"
   - (4) A shoe box with a torn up TV guide
   - (5) A notebook with outlined notes or a mind-map of notes
   - (6) A light bulb
   - (7) A highlighter pen
   - (8) A small clock
   - (9) An eraser
   - (10) A pack of note cards
   - (11) Items of your choice
   - (12) Items of your choice

B. Student teams will seek out the clues for 5-10 minutes. At the end of the search time, the team will study the clues it has gathered and try to identify the missing person (a successful student). If no team is successful, all the clues are brought together for study by the entire search team.

    (1) What are the clues?

    (2) How can we group these using our past experience?

    (3) What do the groups and subgroups say about the missing person?

METACOGNITIVE DISCUSSION

1. How did you go about arranging the clues?

2. What threw you off track?

3. What helped you make your decision about the identity of the missing person?

4. Retrace the steps you went through to make your decision.

5. How good a detective are you? What skills do you need to sharpen?

6. Compare how you generally go about drawing conclusions from facts with the thinking steps you used here.

CLOSURE

In your LOG, outline the steps that work best for you when you have to draw conclusions. Highlight the pitfalls that you have to avoid.

FISHBONE

BACKGROUND

Put your finger on a flame, and you will burn your finger. Put a nail in a tire, and you will get a flat. Cause and effect relationships are visible all around us. There are also more complex effects that puzzle us: what caused a car to crash, a shuttle to explode, the heat to turn off? These require more intense and careful study, some of which will require facts and figures to supply the proof. By using the fishbone pattern as a cause-effect analysis tool, we can speed the diagnostic process.

THINKING SKILL: ANALYZING CAUSE & EFFECT

FOCUS ACTIVITY

To introduce the words cause and effect. Define both words and provide examples of each on the board.

CAUSE:

DEFINITION: That which makes an event happen.

EXAMPLE: A lit cigarette tossed into a gas puddle.

EFFECT:

DEFINITION: That which results from an action taken.

EXAMPLE: The gas explodes.

Ask students to express the definition in their own words and to add other examples.

OBJECTIVE

To use the fishbone pattern to identify and to analyze the causes of a problem.

INPUT

Begin by reviewing the concept of analysis (the breaking of a concept into its parts in order to show relationships of parts to the whole) and by reviewing examples and uses for analysis.

On the board or overhead, draw and explain a fishbone pattern.

like the bones   like the head

Indicate that this pattern will help them organize their thoughts as they analyze causes and effects. In the fishbone box, enter a sample problem (i.e. dirty dishes in sink) and the four major category labels: machine, method, materials, and manpower.

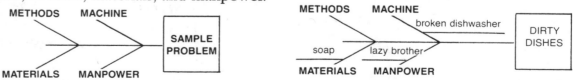

Ask individuals to provide you with causes of the sample problem. For instance, if "dirty dishes" is the problem, broken dishwasher could fit under machine, bad soap under materials, my lazy brother under manpower, etc.

FISHBONE

Invite several students to give other sample causes and the category in which to list the causes. After you have marked in the responses, summarize the process, key definitions (cause, effect) and check for understanding.

ACTIVITY   Instructions:

1. Divide the class into groups of five. Assign the leader, materials manager, recorder, timekeeper and observer roles. Give each group markers, tape and newsprint on which to sketch a giant fishbone.

2. Using response in turn to ensure that all contribute equally, each group will fill out the fishbone. (5 minutes)

3. After the possible causes are listed, members should *clarify* the listed effects. (10 minutes)

4. After clarifying, each group member may select the three listed items which best meet these criteria:

    A. Clearest evidence exists (we can measure it)
    B. Strongest evidence exists (most able to stand alone)

5. On a second chart, list each selected cause. All who selected the cause in #4 may add arguments in favor of the selection. Repeat the listing of arguments for all selected causes.

CAUSE	RATIONALE

6. After the discussion, give each person in the group a "3 vote" for the #1 choice, a "2" and a "1." Tally the weighted votes and create a rank order of selected causes.

METACOGNITIVE DISCUSSION

1. Identify the #1 choice in each group. List these on the board or overhead.

2. Ask each group (a) to explain the rationale for its #1 choice, (b) how well the choice met the criteria and, most importantly, (c) the proof that would be used to support the criteria. Push for clarification of thinking.

CLOSURE   Have each group to decide how it would gather factual data to support its cause-effect selection. The plan should describe *what* data they would collect and *how* they would collect it.

THE OTHER SIDE OF THE COIN

BACKGROUND One of the most cited intelligent behaviors is the ability of a critically thinking person to examine both sides of key issues. What are the strengths and the weaknesses of an argument? What are the positive results and the negative consequences? The benefits and the drawbacks? The pluses and minuses? Very often, students display "unintelligent behavior" by looking only at one side of the issue. It's either all positive or all negative. They find it hard to think that any issue can have both pluses and minuses.

THINKING SKILL: EXAMINING OPPOSITE POINTS OF VIEW

FOCUS ACTIVITY On the overhead or board, draw a positive (+) negative (—) question (?) chart.

ISSUE:		
+	—	?

Take a current issue that has interest to your students (i.e. a school rule forbidding after school jobs, a requirement of a "C" average to play sports, a required rule for ½ an hour of homework per class). Following DOVE, brainstorm a list of positives for that rule. When you have enough items, brainstorm the negatives. End by brainstorming interesting questions raised by the issue. These questions will occur when the students are not sure about some aspect of the issue and want to find out more about that issue.

OBJECTIVE To examine opposite points of view.

INPUT Most of us have strong views on many topics. That is good! It is better if we not only hold a view, but if we can back up our view with facts and logic. What is best is that we have thought through the ideas and solidified our point of view by examining the issue from all sides. (Give an example or two from your own experience.)

Sadly, however, all of us don't look back at both sides of the coin. Many persons, for instance, pick up a point of view from a friend (i.e. "I tried drugs; nothing happened; they can't hurt you" or other examples from your experience) and never question or examine the idea. Perhaps, the most important reason for studying any idea from a different point of view is that a solid investigation helps us understand, rather than merely accept an idea blindly. With understanding comes stronger commitment. (Give another example from your own experience.)

ACTIVITY Instructions:

1. Divide students into groups of three. Give each group a newspaper story or news magazine story. The stories you select would best describe a controversial action taken by a person.

THE OTHER SIDE OF THE COIN

2. Instruct one student to read the story quietly to the group. The others will take notes to identify the controversy.

3. Give each group a sheet of newsprint and a marker. Project the chart on the overhead for them to copy.

4. Instruct the groups to enter the issue and brainstorm each column (+,—,?) as you did in the focus activity. They must have responses in each column.

METACOGNITIVE DISCUSSION

1. What was easy to think about in this task?

2. What was difficult?

3. How can thinking about issues benefit from this approach with the +,—,? chart?

CLOSURE Ask each student to reflect on one instance in which he or she might use this chart to study an issue in his or her own lives. (You may want to brainstorm more issues from school, peer groups, etc. for them.) Give each a chance to share why he or she selected the issue and how the chart might help.

BLIND MEN AND ELEPHANTS

BACKGROUND Analysis for bias is a difficult skill to master. Bias is often hidden within the subtleties of written material, under the surface of glossy advertising or beneath the passion of deeply held beliefs. We are served 'instant-news' from all corners of the world as it is still happening. We are bombarded with slick testimonials for a milieu of commercially appealing products. We are witnesses to live political debates meticulously manipulated to present the most favorable impressions. We face a deluge of printed material; newspapers presenting local and national items, covering a broad scope of interests; magazines highlighting particular and varied special interest areas. In short, we are part and parcel of a 'media-mania' world. How do we know what to believe? EOIOC? guides students into critical thinking: gathering facts, sorting data, proving or justifying data and advocating their 'reasoned conclusions.'

Critical thinkers will *not* believe everything they hear and read. They will step back, review the data systematically, look for telling clues through a line by line, piece by piece search, match clue patterns to an ideal or standard and make a critical judgment based on this analysis.

Bias is not necessarily a negative component, for bias is rooted in belief and conviction:

"There are only two ways to be quite unprejudiced and impartial. One is to be completely ignorant. The other is to completely indifferent. Bias and prejudice are attitudes to be kept in hand, not attitudes to be avoided."

Charles P. Curtis

Thus, as critical thinkers, we need to be aware of possible biases in the material we're exposed to, for only in thorough examination of data are we able to make judgments based on fact and advocate opinions based on sound reason.

THINKING SKILL: ANALYSIS FOR BIAS

FOCUS ACTIVITY Place this figure on the chalkboard.

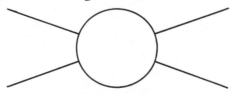

Mentally divide the class into three groups, giving each group cards with the directions written below. Instruct students: "Read your directions. Do not discuss them with anyone. Make your sketches privately. Get started, now. You'll have about 5 minutes."

Directions:

Group 1: Use the design and visualize an object coming *STRAIGHT AT YOU.* Draw your idea.

Group 2: Use the design and visualize an object *DIRECTLY ABOVE YOU.* Draw your idea.

Group 3: Use the design and visualize an object *DIRECTLY BENEATH YOU.* Draw your idea.

After students have completed their drawings, ask them to tape their drawings up on the wall. Allow time for observation, then process the idea of how different point of views influence the way we look at objects - (and drawings).

BLIND MEN AND ELEPHANTS

| OBJECTIVE | To use critical analogies to identify bias. |

INPUT — Provide students with the following:

1. A definition of bias.

2. Synonyms for bias: prejudice, exaggeration, over-generalization, imbalance, opinion, "charged" words.

3. Explanations and examples of the synonyms.

4. The EOIOC Model for bias clues:

> **E** = Exaggeration ("Never," "Always")
> **O** = Over-Generalization
> **I** = Imbalance (One sided story)
> **O** = Opinion as FACT ("They say")
> **C** = Charged Words ("Any jerk knows")

ACTIVITY — Instructions:

1. Read or tell the story in your own words "The Blind Men and The Elephant"

   1st touched *side* - It's like a *wall."*
   2nd touched *tail* - "It's like a *rope."*
   3rd touched *tusk* - "It's like a *sword."*
   4th touched *leg* - "It's like a *tree."*
   5th touched *ear* - "It's like a *fan."*

METACOGNITIVE DISCUSSION

1. What *points of view* are presented? Explain why they are so varied.
2. Give some examples of *exaggeration.*
3. How does this story illustrate *imbalance*?
4. Why were there so many instances of *over-generalization*?
5. Give some examples of "charged words" — if you recall any — from this story?
6. Do you think the distortions were intentional? Why or why not?
7. Does *intent* in bias make a difference? Why or why not?
8. What would you do if you were blind and wanted to investigate the elephant differently?

CLOSURE — In the LOG, complete one of these stems:

- Some steps to consider when analyzing for bias are...
- Analyzing for bias is like...
- When analyzing for bias, I learned that I...
- Some bias words I use are...

PAPA

BACKGROUND In the previous lesson, students were introduced to bias and the EOIOC Model. This lesson will build on that model so that students can practice looking for "bias clues" in an orderly process by identifying bias patterns or a connected sequence of clues.

THINKING SKILL: IDENTIFYING BIAS PATTERNS

FOCUS ACTIVITY Assign students a story from a magazine, newspaper or the language arts text. Before they begin, give them background about the source of the story and ask them to predict any bias they might find. On the board, write a large "P" and record the *predictions*. Next, instruct them to review and use EOIOC to analyze the story for bias clues.

Exaggeration
Over-generalization
Imbalance
Opinion stated as fact
Charged words

After the reading is done, write a giant "A" on the board and record their clue samples next to it. When you have completed the *analysis*, mark a second "P" on the board. Invite students to *prove*, or give evidence from the document to support EOIOC. Finally, mark a second "A" and ask students to *advocate* a conclusion which identifies the bias pattern.

OBJECTIVE Analyzing bias patterns.

INPUT Explain "PAPA" to the class:

P = predict
A = analyze
P = prove
A = advocate

Solicit examples of each from the task just completed.

ACTIVITY

Instructions:

1. Assign students to trios. In each trio, be sure there is a recorder, a leader and an observer.

2. Invite each trio to select one item from each column below:

A	B
black slave	freedom
Yankee general	slavery
slave trader	wealth
plantation owner	fear
northern carpet bagger	

   Check for understanding of all terms.

3. The trio will compose either an editorial, TV news interview or a news story. They will address the topic (Column B) from the point of view of the person (Column A) and use at least 3 bias clues of EⓄIⓄC to establish a bias pattern. Allow 10 minutes.

4. The trios will exchange stories. The new trio will use PAPA to identify the pattern. Allow 5 minutes.

5. Join the trios together (sixes) to report on PAPA to each other.

METACOGNITIVE DISCUSSION

1. Ask students to respond orally to these stems:

   A. Bias is good because...
   B. Bias is bad because...
   C. I'm aware of bias when...

2. Extend responses without judgement.

CLOSURE

Distribute a 3″ X 5″ card to each student. Ask each to complete this stem: "A question I have about bias is..." or "A way I can use PAPA is..." Collect and read anonymous samples of each.

COURT ROOM

BACKGROUND   When students are learning to analyze for bias, they need much practice in applying EOIOC and PAPA to the subtleties of language. There are many situations in which they will read or hear biased statements: The substance abuser who is sure "everyone does it"; the neighbor who thinks that "those people ruin our neighborhood"; the lawyer who argues the facts from one point of view; the editorial that takes one side. Perhaps no place gives a better chance to consider bias than situations related to politics, government and law. Analytic thinkers who can hear and dissect bias will make stronger citizens.

THINKING SKILL: ANALYZING FOR BIAS

FOCUS ACTIVITY   Using a well-known fairytale such as *The Three Little Pigs*, elicit a retelling of the tale by students. After refreshing memories with the 'facts' of the story, give these instructions: "B. D. Wolf is coming to trial. He has been indicted on three counts: property destruction, vandalism and public disturbance. Your job today is to select an unbiased jury to hear the case. Those of you on this side of the room will vote on possible jurors. Those of you on that side of the room will be assigned roles to play in the legal proceedings."

OBJECTIVE   To identify biased arguments.

INPUT   Hand out card (underlined only) to each student. Ask the class to comment on the responsibilities of each role. After this discussion, make the connection to the story (in parentheses).

1. *Defense attorney:* (You will represent Wolf)

2. *State appointed Prosecutor:* (You will represent Pig's family.)

3. *Judge:* (You will preside over proceedings.)

4. *Educator:* (You teach little piggies.)

5. *Lady Skunk:* (Animal kingdom *always* shuns you.)

6. *Cab Driver:* (You, too live in a small 'tiny' cottage.)

7. *Bank President:* (Piggies need loan to rebuild.)

8. *Land Baron:* (You want piggies' land.)

9. *Local Contractor:* (You might get job to rebuild houses.)

10. *High Rise Dweller:* (You can't relate to "cottage" dweller.)

11. *Bailiff:* (You keep order and escort prospects in and out.)

12. *Court Recorder:* (You write down proceedings.)

13. *Court Reporter:* (You're looking for a story.)

14. *Court Clerk:* (You swear in prospective jurors and say "all rise" as judge enters.)

15. *Policeman:* (You are on police force in another town.)

16. *Other*

ACTIVITY

1. ***Instructions to the role-players out in the hall:*** "You will use as many *bias clues* as you can while being interviewed. *Exaggerate! Oversimplify!* Show an *imbalance* in your feelings about things that might show bias on the case, assert *opinion* as fact and use "emotion-*charged*" words. Remember, you have a role to play. Do not let your personal feelings enter in. Represent the point of view of your assigned role. Think about your role while I give the other's their instructions."

2. ***Instructions to audience:*** (while prospective jurors are out of hearing range.) "Those of you who will be voting on jurors have a difficult task. Your *goal* is to select *six* jurors. Your criteria is simply to find those candidates you feel demonstrate the *least bias* toward the case. You will use the *Bias Clue Sheet* as you listen to the proceedings."

JURORS / CLUES	Example	Skunk	Cabbie	Bank President	Land Baron	Local Contributor	High Rise Dweller	Educator	Policeman	Other	NOTES
Exaggeration	II										
Over-Generalization	I										
Imbalance	I										
Opinion as Fact	III										
Charged Words	I										
TOTALS	8										

COURT ROOM

"Each time a prospective juror reveals a *bias clue* during the selection proceedings, make a mark in the proper box. For example, if the cabbie describes his "twig" house that he has *slaved* all his life for, you might mark, "charged words" because of the emotional word "slaved." A bias for the pigs' predicament is suspected. You may want to make notes on the side of the sheet for later reference.

At the end of the selection process, the six characters with the lowest score will be selected. However, either attorney can reject any prospective juror.

3. *Instructions to the Court Personnel in room:*

"You are playing roles of people who work in the courts. Be professional, assume the identity of your role and act accordingly. Any questions?"

4. *Instructions for Role-Playing: Jury Selection*

The prospective jurors are called to the stand and interviewed by both attorneys. Either attorney can reject a prospective juror. If a juror is rejected, *no reason* is given and the person is dismissed at that time.

Ironic note: Each attorney develops a "bias profile" of jurors he feels will be most *sympathetic to his client's point of view.* As he interviews, he is actually interviewing for *no* bias.

5. Rearrange room as needed. Reassemble all students in the room and begin proceedings. (Since the attorneys are key to the proceedings, select those roles carefully, choosing students who can ad-lib and carry-on quite well in this sort of simulation.) Proceed through all prospective jurors following simulated court procedures. Use role definition as a guide to courtroom behaviors.

After the final candidate is interviewed, each student should tally his *Bias Clue Sheet.*

COURT ROOM

METACOGNITIVE DISCUSSION

Do a class tally of the *Bias Clue Sheet*. Remember, the *six* characters with the smallest numbers tallied are the jurors selected by the unbiased audience - even if some of those same people have been dismissed by the attorneys.

1. How was bias most frequently revealed? (EOIOC)

2. Is it possible to be a totally unbiased juror?

3. How do attorneys finally select the jurors? How do they weigh the criteria?

4. Describe some *non-verbal clues* of *bias*.

5. Who appeared most *flagrantly* biased? Why do you think so? What clues did you detect?

6. Who appeared most *unbiased* of all? Why?

7. Describe a "profile of bias" from the State Attorney's point of view, and the Defense Attorney's point of view.

CLOSURE

Write LOG entries about *bias:*

A *positive* aspect of *bias* is...

A *negative* aspect of *bias* is...

An *intriguing* aspect of *bias* is...

A HUMAN BIAS GRAPH

BACKGROUND Some more practice for bias. In this case, the activity will help students identify some of their own biases. They will get the chance not only to analyze their bias, but also to evaluate their positions.

THINKING SKILL: EVALUATING BIAS

FOCUS ACTIVITY Make a *HUMAN GRAPH*. Stand in the center of the room and have students cluster in front of you. Draw an imaginary line dividing the space into segments (or place masking tape on the floor with the appropriate markings). Assign *degrees of agreement* to indicate intensity of convictions (Outline on the board for quick reference).

WILLING TO DIE IN AGREEMENT	NEUTRAL	WILLING TO DIE IN DISAGREEMENT

Ask students to move on the graph in response to each statement.

1. Honesty is the best policy! (Cervantes)
2. The only way to have a friend is to be one. (Emerson)
3. Music is the universal language of mankind. (Longfellow)
4. The pen is mightier than the sword. (Bulver-Rytton)

Pose the question as you indicate the side for each choice. Watch as they move to one side or the other. Then *ask why? LISTEN!* Permit time for each volunteer to explain his decision. *Wait!*

OBJECTIVE To evaluate our biases.

INPUT Using the example from the focus activity where there was the most disagreement on the graph, construct a +/— chart on the board or overhead. List first all the arguments in support of the position (+). Secondly, list the arguments against (—). Review EOIOC.

Exaggeration
Over-generalization
Imbalance
Opinion stated as fact
Charged words

and PAPA:
Predict point of view; possible bias
Analyze 'EOIOC'; look for bias clues
Prove: Find evidence of 'EOIOC'; document
Advocate: Justify a conclusion or opinion based on your search.

with the +/— chart to pinpoint bias clues and bias patterns on both sides.

POSITION

+	—

A HUMAN BIAS GRAPH

ACTIVITY   Instructions:

1. Divide students into groups of three. Give each group one of the following:

    a. a famous quote
    b. a news story or editorial
    c. lyrics of a current hit song

    or have them watch together:

    a. a talk show
    b. a news report
    c. a TV documentary that you video taped

2. Each group will analyze the material and decide to what degree they agree or disagree with the major ideas.

3. Each group will use a piece of newsprint to list 3-5 arguments in support of their position (agree or disagree).

4. Each group will join with 2 other groups to analyze the arguments for their bias. (Use EᎮIᎮC and PAPA) where biased statements were identified, the original trio will make changes to remove the bias and construct a new list.

METACOGNITIVE DISCUSSION

1. Identify in what ways you revealed bias in your arguments.

2. How did you change the arguments to eliminate the bias?

3. In thinking about the ways you argue with your parents, friends or fellow students, what are the more typical bias patterns you show?

4. How helpful are your bias patterns? Harmful?

5. What are some ways you can improve your arguments without using bias patterns?

CLOSURE   Realign students for a human graph. Ask them to respond to the following:

1. Some bias is good.

2. The TV news is always biased.

3. It's important to know our biases.

After students move on the graph, ask for volunteers to explain their reasons.

A BUY YOU CAN'T REFUSE

BACKGROUND Every time we pick up an ad, we are challenged to identify the hidden message. The hidden message is built on an assumption. For instance, an ad might say: "Buy the Large Economy Size." The ad is telling us to accept the assumption that the large size will save us money. It doesn't say anything about buying more product than we need or that the box may really be larger but have no more product in it than a competitor's smaller box. Do we accept the statement and buy the large economy size, or do we check out the facts carefully?

THINKING SKILL: ANALYZING FOR ASSUMPTIONS

FOCUS ACTIVITY Place the following signs in different corners of the room.

a. Strongly Agree   **b.** Mildly Agree   **c.** Mildly Disagree   **d.** Strongly Disagree

Tell the class that you are going to announce a series of assumptions that you hold to be correct. After each thinks about the statement, he or she will move to the corner that best represents his/her position on the statement. After students have moved to the corners, you may wish to ask for sample rationales.

a. Women are more necessary to the well being of this society than men.

b. If teenagers are old enough at 18 to fight, they are old enough to drink.

c. The government that governs least is the government that governs best.

OBJECTIVE To develop methods to analyze unwarranted claims and broad assertions for their false assumptions.

INPUT On the board or overhead, define the word assumption: an unproven claim, a broad assertion without proof or a generalization that lacks specific backup. Provide examples from ads such as the following:

a. *Claim:* "People who know...go Bird Airways."
Assumption: If you don't fly this airline, you are not one of the smart people.

b. *Claim:* "You can buy audio and video at a lot of stores, but only Jones audio gives you perfection."
Assumption: If you don't buy from this store, you take a chance on buying a defective product.

A BUY YOU CAN'T REFUSE

Outline for the students the 6 ASSUME guidelines

1. **A**ssume assertions are present.

2. **S**earch deliberately for the hidden messages.

3. **S**ense gaps in logic.

4. **U**se linking statements to check validity.

5. **M**ake revisions to clarify.

6. **E**xpress revised statement.

Use the following example to illustrate how they can use the guidelines. "YOU CAN NEVER BE TOO ORGANIZED. So we have constructed the perfect wallet that guarantees you'll always know where your most important items are. Let us save you time and money with the Ultimate Time Saver Wallet."

1. "The wallet looks great, but I need to think about this ad. My past experience tells me that there isn't anything that is perfect."

2. "I am going to look first for all the sweeping generalizations. My clues will be words such as "all," "always," "never," "everybody," "most," "best" and other superlatives. (Work through and underline each one you find.)

3. "For each underlined word, I want to know where the proof is provided." Does my experience hold this claim to be true? Is there some data or a reliable source to back this up? Do I believe the source? (For instance, ask out loud, "how organized do I need to be? Is there any validity to the claim about never being too organized?"

4. On the board or overhead, write a few sample links: (i.e. "Can I ever be too organized?" "Yes, when..." or "Am I unorganized?" "No." or "Will all my most important items fit in this wallet." "No, my children won't.") Ask the students to make links for some of the other assumptions.

5. Revise the ad. (Do this on the board or overhead so the students can see you making the changes.

6. The revised statement: "Sometimes it helps to have a wallet that organizes the items you think are important to carry in a wallet. If you use the compartments well, you will have a better chance of finding what you want, when you need it. Check out this wallet to see that it has the compartments that you need."

Check for understanding about the six guidelines so that students can explain each in their own words.

A BUY YOU CAN'T REFUSE

ACTIVITY   Instructions:

1. Divide the class into pairs. Provide each pair with a newspaper or magazine. Tell the pair to select an ad to analyze. They will use the 6 ASSUME Guidelines. (10 minutes.)

2. After they have completed the task, each pair will match with a second pair. The first pair will share its ad analysis. When the first pair is finished , the second pair will share its analysis. If either needs assistance or questions the other's logic, they should discuss until the time expires. Be sure both teams have a chance to share. (10 minutes.)

A BUY YOU CAN'T REFUSE

METACOGNITIVE DISCUSSION Keep the students in the groups of four. Assign a recorder, an observer, leader and timekeeper for this 15 minute task to which all must contribute.

Provide this chart for the group to complete.

ASSUMPTION KEY	QUESTION	FACTS	EXPERIENCE	EXPERTISE

In Column 1, list the key words you used to identify the assumptions.
In Column 2, list the question you asked to check the assumptions.
In Column 3, list the facts you used to invalidate the assumptions.
In Column 4, list personal experiences you used to invalidate the assumptions.
In Column 5, list the expertise you used to invalidate the assumptions.

After charts are complete, ask the students to discuss what they found difficult about analyzing for assumptions. How might they ease these difficulties? Make a list of "What to do if..." ideas that they can record in the LOG and conclude by discussing situations other than ads in which they might put the ASSUME guidelines to work (i.e. listening to speakers, reading an editorial, etc.).

CLOSURE Instruct each student to pick an object they can see in the classroom (pencil, flower vase, tack, etc.). In their LOGS, they should create some headline statements that advertise the object. The statements should contain some assumption errors. If there is time, share and identify the errors.

PROVE IT!

BACKGROUND   Reports from the National Assessment Tests* indicate that upper-grade students are not doing well when it comes to finding and giving proof to back up an argument or a concept. There are several possible reasons.

1. Teachers are too caught up in the use of multiple choice tests that ask students only to pick out facts or select the main idea. They are not pushing students to the next level and asking students to justify with proof.

OR

2. If students are being asked to give proof, they are doing so only with the material in front of them. They are not aware of any specific methods they might use to find proof, nor do they consciously think about how they do make their selections.

OR

3. The students do think consciously through the methods and mental processes inherent in finding proof, but they do not transfer their metacognition to new and different problems because they do not know how to make such applications.

OR

4. A combination of the above.

*For proof of contention and for data to review about the possible readings, see the discussion of National Assessment Tests in the Introduction.

THINKING SKILL: ANALYZING FOR PROOF

FOCUS ACTIVITY   Give to each student a copy of this article about the Challenger accident. Ask them to read it carefully. When they are finished, list and discuss the responses to the following sequence of questions.

1. What conclusions were drawn about the accident?

2. What proof or evidence is given to back up each conclusion?

3. Give your reasons to argue why the evidence given is sufficient proof for the conclusion.

4. On the basis of this discussion, how much proof would you say is enough proof?

OBJECTIVE   To identify methods for finding and giving sufficient proof.

SHUTTLE CABIN HIT SEA INTACT

CAPE CANAVERAL, Fla. - The crew cabin of the space shuttle Challenger plunged nearly nine miles and crashed into the Atlantic Ocean virtually intact, a top federal safety investigator said Wednesday.

Based on debris recovered during salvage operations, Terry J. Armentrout, director of the National Transportation Safety Board's Bureau of Accident Investigation, said the debris from the shuttle's orbiter "indicates that the [orbiter] shell did not fall off by itself."

"It had to have some mass inside," he said. "Obviously, that mass is the crew module."

Armentrout's statements mark the first official determination that the orbiter did not explode 73 seconds into flight in a midair fireball January 28, raising new questions about when and how the seven aboard the shuttle were killed and whether any safety features could have saved them from the worst disaster in space history.

Thousands who watched the doomed launch both here and on television initially thought that the orbiter had exploded, along with the shuttle's huge external fuel tank and solid rocket boosters. NASA officials also said they believed that the shuttle's crew was killed instantly.

But Armentrout said Wednesday that based on the lack of fire damage on the recovered segments of the orbiter, it would appear the crew compartment did not explode. In fact, he said, despite the fireball there was no major explosion of any shuttle component.

The fire most likely could be explained by a volatile mix of escaping hydrogen and oxygen. He said it appeared that the orbiter had broken away from the huge external fuel tank before it could be severely damaged by the fire.

He refused to address the question of when and how the astronauts, including schoolteacher Christa McAuliffe, died, but noted that only the orbiter's tail and part of its right wing showed any significant fire damage.

Other officials have said there is virtually no way the astronauts could have withstood the aerodynamic forces involved in the orbiter's 8.9 - mile tumbling fall.

Armentrout said that the orbiter suffered some aerodynamic damage in its plunge from the sky, and significant water-impact damage, but no fire damage.

"The term explosion has been used a long time," Armentrout said. "And of course there was evidence of explosion visually. But an explosion of the entire shuttle is not something we are seeing."

Early in the investigation, videotapes of the launch showed a large, and then unexplained, piece of debris crashing into the Atlantic Ocean off Cape Canaveral. Some investigators speculated at the time that the debris was the orbiter.

Some pieces of the orbiter's outer shell floated on the ocean surface just days after the accident, but the bulk of the crew compartment and remains of the astronauts were not recovered for more than a month.

Wednesday's disclosures, coupled with earlier recovery of crew remains, are sure to fuel more talk about whether the shuttle was adequately equipped with safety features, such as an escape mechanism.

The first two shuttle missions, for example, had ejection seats. Those were abandoned to cut costs and decrease weight so that the shuttle could transport more commercial payloads.

Wednesday, for the first time publicly, NASA allowed reporters to view some of the debris.

The tangled debris was displayed on wooden sawhorses in a cavernous hangar at the Kennedy Space Center. Barnacles still clung to many shuttle pieces.

The recovered portions of the shuttle lay in neat, organized configurations, tagged for identification and many appeared surprisingly intact.

This contrasted sharply with early theories that large segments were shattered during the initial fire.

The debris is important for investigators as they attempt to pinpoint precisely the cause of the accident and discuss modifications of the shuttle in the wake of the accident.

So far, Armentrout said, some critical shuttle parts, namely key portions of the right solid rocket booster, have not been found.

NASA investigators and members of the presidential commission investigating the accident have all but concluded that a failure near a crucial field joint of the shuttle allowed super hot gases to escape and triggered the accident.

On Tuesday, the manager of NASA's internal investigation for the first time admitted that the booster rocket's joint was flawed and that the space agency had not paid enough attention to previous problems.

J.R. Thompson, the vice chairman of NASA's internal review board, said his board will present additional findings to members of the presidential commission investigating the accident Thursday at the Marshall Space Flight Center, in Huntsville, Ala.

Commission members have said that their final report will contain a recommendation that the suspect joints that hold the rocket booster segments together be completely redesigned.

PROVE IT!

INPUT Using the article as an example, discuss with the class how often it is necessary to draw conclusions from evidence. In most cases, as with the Challenger, it is very difficult to come up with the exact, 100% correct answer. We must try to come as close as we can. We must have what is called "sufficient proof."

Review with the class the difference between "soft data" and "hard data."

> *SOFT DATA:* Opinions, bias, personal views. We must subject soft data to additional analysis. What are the facts behind the opinions? Can we support the opinion with logical, sensible arguments? For instance, in the article, Mr. Armentrout says: "The debris *indicates* that the shell did not fall off by itself." His argument is logical, but he suggests that he doesn't have enough hard data to prove his point.

> *HARD DATA:* Facts that we can observe and measure and in sufficient quantity to show that a statistically reliable pattern exists. For instance, if a custodian went to every classroom in this building and counted exactly 27 seats per room, he could say: "Every classroom has the same number of seats." When asked for proof, he could say: "I counted them. Here are the count sheets."

In every case, we cannot be 100% accurate with the proof. However, we can look for as much proof as we can find to back up our statements. Then, like the investigators in the Challenger accident, we must modify what we say. If...

We are less than 100% sure but have hard data to use as proof, then we can say, "maybe, in some cases, a few, suggests, or seems."

When we are constructing our own arguments it is important that we follow five "PROVE" rules:

1. **P**ick as much data as we can for evidence.

2. **R**eview the data to make sure it supports our case logically.

3. **O**rganize the data to show the pattern.

4. **V**alidate the data by checking for its accuracy.

5. **E**valuate the reliability of your data source.

After you have outlined the PROVE rules, which students should note in their LOGS, demonstrate the use of the five rules by walking through the Challenger news article and showing how the evidence given does or does not back up conclusions stated and identify what additional data is needed. Conclude by asking several different students to explain the rules in their own way and to give examples of their own.

ACTIVITY Instructions:

1. Divide the class into teams of three. Appoint a leader, recorder and timekeeper. Give each team a copy of the "Clues Told In Crash Of GI Charter" article (or substitute one of your own).

CLUES TOLD IN CRASH OF GI CHARTER

The plane, a charter flight operated by Arrow Air Inc., carried a crew of 8 and 248 members of the U.S. Army's elite 101st Airborne Division who were returning to Ft. Campbell, Ky., for Christmas after a tour of duty as a peacekeeping force in the Sinai Desert.

Those conclusions, based on 10 reports by investigators were that the airplane was fatigued from 51,000 hours of flying, and that several factors could have contributed to the crash.

"We are considering combinations [of possible causes whose] cumulative effects could - and I emphasize could - prove significant," Boag said.

They include several complications relayed by the crew during a refueling stop in Cologne, West Germany, and in Cairo, before the flight.

Among factors that may have contributed to the crash:

• The plane was carrying 1,700 pounds more weight than the flight crew had calculated, which may have decreased takeoff speed.

• Possible ice formation on the wings after the plane landed in Gander could have affected the takeoff. Boag, however, cautioned, "There is no evidence there was or was not ice on the wings."

• The No. 4 engine may have been running at an extremely low speed. At one point it was reported to have been running much hotter than the three other engines. Boag said this engine had been used so long that it was scheduled to be retired at the end of that trip.

• An elevator control, which controls the plane's lift and drop, may have been defective.

Witnesses told investigators the plane took off from runway No. 22, and passed over the Trans-Canada Highway at an altitude of 100 feet.

From there, the plane seemed to level off, they said, then lost power and banked to an angle of about 14 degrees. With its right wing lowered, the plane hit treetops 2,973 feet from the end of the runway.

On its flight from the Middle East, the plane was examined in Cairo and in Cologne.

Reports examined by Boag's investigators show that the Arrow Air crew worried about several problems, including excess baggage that they feared might block the emergency exits.

They reported that every overhead rack and closet was filled, and that passengers sat with their feet atop bags that wouldn't fit under the seats.

Some of the other problems reported during the trip:

• Some control panel lights weren't working and warning indicators clicked on for no reason.

• Fluid was leaking from the right landing gear.

• A passenger saw fire leap from an engine on the left wing.

• The forward cargo door was stuck and the crew finally opened it "using a fire-ax and then a pocketknife."

• Passengers complained that the windows and some paneled areas were sealed with duct tape, cold air was leaking through the front passenger door, and the air-craft's water systems were leaking.

When the plane reached Cologne, flight attendants reported that the washroom floors were "unusually soft or squishy."

PROVE IT!

2. Instruct the leader in each team to read the article aloud to the team.

3. Give each team a sheet of newsprint, markers and tape. On the overhead or board display the model that they are to copy.

CONCLUSION:

PROOF:	RELIABLE SOURCE	HARD DATA
1.		
2.		
3.		
4.		

METACOGNITIVE DISCUSSION After the teams have finished their charts, tape the charts around the room. Allow the students to mill around the room and examine the charts. If they find a chart which they feel is using the wrong or insufficient data as proof, they should write down their questions.

When students are reseated, discuss the following:

1. Are there any charts which you think are using data that does not prove the point? (Focus on one example at a time. Be sure the challenger argues his/her case and then allow the author team to change or correct its chart, or defend its case.)

2. When you were thinking about the evidence you would use to make your case, what was the most difficult part of the thinking you had to do? What was the easiest thinking you had to do? (Be aware that what was difficult for one was easy for another. When this occurs, ask the students to comment on why that would be so.)

3. If you were to redo this investigation, how might you approach it differently in the way you think about finding proof?

CLOSURE Instruct students to read a short story, a short biography or a character description. Tell them to form a conclusion about the reading and to select proof to support their case. (Using the PROVE rules.) Finally, they are to make a chart in which they illustrate how they used the five rules in their own thinking about the assigned reading. Post these around the classroom and use them for a follow-up discussion.

NOTES

THE TOWER TEST

BACKGROUND In every aspect of our lives, we are being judged. In sports, in school work and on-the-job, standards are set or we pick criteria to measure performance and make selections. Very often the criteria or measuring sticks are clear. Just as often, they are hidden or unknown. Skillful thinkers learn to identify criteria so that they can make more effective decisions.

THINKING SKILL: IDENTIFYING CRITERIA

FOCUS ACTIVITY On a table or desk in the front of the room, place the following objects (or substitute your own): a candy bar, a milk carton, a carrot, and a sugar packet. Ask for several different volunteers to come up and select one object. After the selection, ask each to write down on a 3 X 5 index card the reason for the selection. When all are done, read the reasons to the class.

OBJECTIVE To identify criteria used in making selections.

INPUT Using the objects selected and the reasons given, demonstrate to students how they used a standard or criterion to make their pick. The criterion may have been easy to measure (vitamin content, size, weight) or more abstract (nutritional value, taste). Whether we were aware of the criterion or not, we still use at least one to make our choices. Skillful thinkers consciously set their criterion as a tool to more effectively think through choices.

Illustrate how often in every day life, criteria are used to make selections (i.e. Professional or College All-Star Teams, Olympic Team Selection, Car of the Year, the stores which are used regularly to buy clothes, food, etc., grading essays and tests).

ACTIVITY Instructions:

1. Divide the class into teams of six. Assign (a) the leader; (b) the cooperative observer (see the chart); and (c) the 4 builders. *The cooperative observer does not build.*

2. Announce that this is a *team* competition. The winning team will be determined by two categories: Product and Cooperation. Each category will have specific criteria.

3. Give each team 3 styrofoam coffee cups, 2 dozen stirrers, 12″ of masking tape and a paper clip. The task is to build a free standing tower using all materials as quickly as possible. All builders must contribute.

4. List the criteria for judging the champion.

   a. Given the use of all materials and contributions by all members, the group will construct 1 free-standing tower.

b. Winners will be judged according to *height* (10 points to the tallest), *stability* (10 points for withstanding the hardest hit), *proportion* (5 points for geometric balance), *attractiveness* (5 points) and *creativity* (5 points). Second, third and fourth in each category will receive 5, 3 and 1 point each. The highest score will win.

c. A second award will go the most cooperative group. For each helpful act or positive statement made by a member, 1 mark will be entered in Column 1 (+). In Coumn 2

	+	−
STUDENT		
A		
B		
C		
D		
E		

d. The team with the best positive total after minuses (−) are deducted wins this award.

5. Start the group task. After 10 minutes, stop all teams and conduct the judging. Also tally the cooperation points. Conclude with the 2 awards.

METACOGNITIVE DISCUSSION

1. What were the criteria for each award?

2. Ask teams to comment on their decisions to emphasize different criteria in the building process.

3. How did the cooperation criteria influence their thinking?

4. What value do they see in knowing clear criteria beforehand?

5. When criteria are not clear, how might they clarify the criteria for a task?

CLOSURE

In the LOG, complete a stem.

Criteria contribute to clear thinking when...

About criteria, it is important that...

Criteria are like _____ because...

TARGET ANALYSIS

BACKGROUND Since the days of Robin Hood, the target has been a symbol for accuracy and sharp sight. Today, the target is a common pattern that visually pinpoints which concepts being studied are most important or central, which are secondary and so forth. Like the archer with a sharp eye and accurate aim, the thinker uses the target for sharp and accurate thinking.

THINKING SKILL: EVALUATING

FOCUS ACTIVITY In the front of the room place a waste can separated by six feet from a chair. Invite a student to sit on the chair and shoot three large paper wads at the basket. Tell the class that the waste can represents a target. Ask the class to identify other targets they have seen or used. For each response, (1) use an attribute web to list it on the board; (2) ask the student to explain how or why the object is a target; and (3) branch hows and whys from the uses.

OBJECTIVE To use the target pattern as a tool to evaluate ideas.

INPUT On the overhead or board, write the following:

1. A definition of target:

2. A visual target:

3. Uses for targets: to score points, to analyze and evaluate ideas, etc.

4. Sample criteria for rings in the target selection:
   A. Center:

most important	key
most valued	most crucial
strong*est*	focus
fi*rst*	_____

108

TARGET ANALYSIS

B.   1st Ring: supporting   backup
                                helpful
                                secondary   _____

C.   2nd Ring: facts   specifics
                                details   _____
                                objects   _____
                                part   _____

5.   A sample target

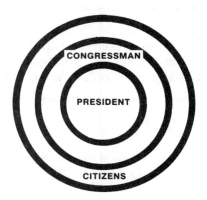

(b) list of names

(a) and criterion

(c) *MOST IMPORTANT*
        IN THE GOVERNMENT

Demonstrate the selection and the necessity of giving reasons for the selections.

ACTIVITY   Instructions:

1. Divide the class into groups of three. Assign roles (recorder, timekeeper, leader) and distribute newsprint and markers.

2. Instruct the recorder to draw a three-ring target.

3. Assign a paragraph or chapter from a textbook, magazine article, or short story to each trio. After they have read the assigned material, have them complete a target analysis according to criteria you provide.

METACOGNITIVE DISCUSSION   1. Describe the content of your reading.

2. Demonstrate and defend your placement of ideas and facts in the target.

3. How would your thinking change if you used a different criterion? Give an example.

4. How precise was your thinking in making the target placements?

5. What was the most difficult thinking required for this task?

CLOSURE   Help students construct a list of academic situations in which they might use the target analysis. Discuss several nominations for the *best* application idea.

RANKING IN ORDER

BACKGROUND A major difference between chaos and confusion vs. order and organization comes from the ability to set priorities. We set criteria and evaluate objects in contrast to each other. The simplest tool to weigh the value among ideas or objects is the rank order. The rank order shows what gets top value, second, third, etc. When tied to our values and beliefs about ideas or objects, it's an effective tool used to force choices.

THINKING SKILL: RANKING IN ORDER

FOCUS ACTIVITY Ask for the names of three popular singers. Write them on the overhead or board. Ask for a student to explain which he likes best, second best, least. Request a different ranking. Next ask a student to predict which of the three will last the longest as a popular singer. Request a different ranking from other students.

OBJECTIVE To use rank order in weighing priorities.

INPUT Rank orders are an evaluation tool used to force choices among priorities. The rankings may be more subjective based on personal values and biases, or more objective, based on measurable facts.

ACTIVITY Instructions:

1. Select three related topics, characters or events from material curently being studied in the course. (i.e. three characters from a short story or three scientists.) Instruct the students to rank order the three by a criterion you provide (i.e. rank order the characters by their importance to the story or by their intergrity. Rank order the scientists by the importance of their contributions to mankind.).

2. Ask individuals to share and explain the rankings given. Note that you want arguments with good evidence, not a single *right* answer.

METACOGNITIVE DISCUSSION

1. When ranking, what criteria or measures did you think about?

2. How important are such criteria when you weigh actions you will take?

3. What effect do rank orders have on how you make judgments?

4. What drawbacks do you find inherent in rank orders.

CLOSURE In your LOG, describe at least one way you could use rank orders as an evaluation tool in your schoolwork.

NOTES

TRUTH OR CONSEQUENCES?

"Truth or Consequences" was a popular radio show which most of us don't remember. When a player failed to answer a question truthfully (the host already knew the answer), he or she was immediately given a "fair" consequence to suffer (pie in the face, water dunking). The show pointed up a universal moral: that consequences or negative results occur. Consequences however, are not limited to acts which we consider negative. They are linked to every action which involves some risk (i.e. driving a car, flying a plane, getting married). Moreover, consequences are not always negative. The risk may end in a positive result (i.e. getting to the moon). Before skillful thinkers elect to act (i.e. buy a product, take a trip, select a college), they weigh the consequences, positive and negative.

THINKING SKILL: WEIGHING CONSEQUENCES

FOCUS ACTIVITY

1. Begin with an all class discussion. Make a list on the board or overhead of "risks" students must take in their everyday lives, (i.e. walk to school). After you have a list of 5-9 items, ask students to explain the seriousness of the risks given (i.e. hit by a car, kidnapped by a stranger, slip on ice). Label these risks negative consequences; or possible bad effects

2. Ask students to list some of the positive consequences or good effects which may come from the risk (i.e. good physical conditioning, save gasoline). Label these positive consequences.

OBJECTIVE To use the plus-minus format as a tool for weighing the consequences of action.

INPUT Outline a plus-minus format on the board or overhead. Select positive and negative consequences from the "risk" lists.

+	−

Define "consequences" and provide students with synonyms. Outline how they can use the format in weighing consequences.

ACTIVITY Instructions:

1. Divide the class into pairs. Instruct each pair to select one of the following situations. In their logs they will construct a plus-minus format and identify the positive and negative consequences of a key choice made by the character. (You may wish to substitute scenarios of your own.)

   A. Mary is in the library. Across the aisle she sees Tom, captain of the varsity football team, rip several pages from the encyclopedia. She decides to follow the school's honor code and tells the librarian what she saw.

B. George is a "second string" debater on the school's team. Sue, a member of the "first string," steals idea cards from a competitor. The stolen cards are reported and George's team faces expulsion from the tournament. Sue, also George's girl friend, confides to George what she did. George decides to keep the secret.

C. Mr. Smith discovers that Al, his first chair violinist in the school orchestra, is selling drugs to other members. It is one week before the all school concert. He decides to confront Al and force Al to either turn himself in or leave the orchestra.

D. Jim has a date with Marion for the Spring Dance. Two nights before the dance, he learns that the baseball coach at State U wants him to visit the campus and talk about a scholarship. He must visit on Saturday and cannot get back to town in time for the dance. He decides to keep the date.

2. After teams have completed the formats, assemble the class for a discussion.

METACOGNITIVE DISCUSSION

1. Select several pairs to share the ideas from their plus-minus formats.

2. Ask "in what situations might you find it helpful to use the plus-minus format?" Seek several responses.

3. What might have happened if (select a literary, historical or current political character familiar to your students) had used a plus-minus format (give the situation)? What would be in the plus column? The minus column?

4. On the board or overhead, map a plus-minus format. Ask the class to give the plus and the minus for using the plus-minus format in making decisions.

CLOSURE In the thinking LOG, invite students to reflect on a situation, action or choice that they are facing in their academic lives (i.e. to go to college, find an afterschool job, etc.) and construct a plus-minus chart.

NOTES

CATCH THEM
THINKING CREATIVELY

THE GUITARGATOR

| **BACKGROUND** | Very often we fail to come up with creative ideas because we fail to look at problems or challenges from a new perspective. When forced to look at different combinations, we often find better solutions. |

THINKING SKILL: FORCING RELATIONSHIPS

| **FOCUS ACTIVITY** | Present the students with these 5 rules for brainstorming: |

1. **B**uild on each others ideas

2. **U**se the far out

3. **I**nvent, invent, invent many answers

4. **L**ist everything and anything

5. **D**o stretch your ideas

ask several students to explain "the key" message behind the five rules and to give examples.

| **OBJECTIVE** | To generate new ideas by forcing new ways to look at familiar objects. |

| **INPUT** | When we are generating new ideas, our tendency is to stay safe and secure in what we perceive is "the right way" or "the acceptable answer." By forcing ouselves to look at old ideas in new ways, we can discover, invent and propose new ideas. BUILD gives us the rules or guidelines, even the mind-set, to stretch our thinking process. Sometimes a strategy such as Guitargator is used as a thinking tool to force us to explore new and different "looks" in advertising and public relations. It also helps writers, artists, and film directors give us a new look. |

| **ACTIVITY** | Instructions: |

1. On the overhead, make two columns. On Column 2, head "animals." On Column 1, head "musical instrument."

2. Following "Build" have students brainstorm each list. Complete 1 before 2. After 1 is full, cover it so that students don't try to match columns. Number each response in each column.

1. MUSICAL INSTRUMENTS	**2. ANIMALS**
1.	1. HORSES
2.	2.
3.	3.
4.	4.
5.	5.
6.	6.
7.	7.
8.	8.
9.	9.
10.	10.
11.	11.
12.	12.

3. From a hat or box with numbered papers from 1-12, ask a student to pick 2 numbers. Circle the numbers on the charts, one from each column.

4. Match the students in random pairs. Give each pair a sheet of newsprint and ask them to sketch a new animal which combines the physical characteristics of both the original animal selected and the musical instrument.

5. Hang the sketches on the front board with a name for the new animal or new musical instrument.

METACOGNITIVE DISCUSSION

1. Ask pairs to identify the new animal or instrument, describe its characteristics, and tell how it might be useful or valuable.

2. Follow-up with questions such as:

    a. What could be the worst possible effect this _____ has on people?

    b. What would happen if you brought a _____ to your house?

    c. How might you respond if someone were to ask you "What were you thinking about when you combined the _____ and the _____ ?"

3. Conclude by describing how important it was to be forced into combining the two objects through a random selection.

CLOSURE

1. Invite students to create an ad for selling this new object to their friends. Give them newsprint, crayons or markers and the rule that the ad must picture the object and use no more than 10 words.
    OR

2. Create an ad slogan to sell the object on a billboard.
    OR

3. Write a jingle about the new object.
    OR

4. Using clay, sculpt the new object.

THE PLANET CREON

BACKGROUND In order to be a skillful creative and critical thinker, one of the skills that has multiple uses is the skill of imaging or visualizing. A thinker who can see "with the mind's eye" is able to reduce issues and problems to a concrete picture. By recreating the concrete, the thinker is able to study the problem from multiple views, analyze the parts and evaluate which thinking skills to use. Metacognitive studies of famous scientists, artist and mathematicians have revealed how and why they are successful thinkers. They have developed the ability to see problems in the concrete, even when the seeing is restricted to creating a visual picture, better than those who remain average thinkers. Recent studies of world class and olympic athletes has corroborated the effectiveness of imaging. Currently, research is focusing on how the athlete can use images to picture a goal, such as a record performance or a gold medal, visualize movement based on memorized motion studies, and retrace one's own movements to reflect these mental pictures.

THINKING SKILL: IMAGING

FOCUS ACTIVITY Ask the students to close their eyes and relax in their seats. Talk them slowly into relaxing. Ask them to use the inside of their eyelids as a movie screen. On the screen, they are to imagine that they are in the gym and that there is no gravity. They should create a movie picture of the gym filled with students and no gravity. What do they see? What are some of the possibilities of things that they could do? What would the wall and floor surfaces look like? What is the gym teacher doing? The students? After a few minutes, call the students to attention. Ask them to share what they imagined in as much detail as possible.

OBJECTIVE To improve imaging as a thinking skill.

INPUT Select a description passage from Conrad's *Lord Jim*. Read it to the class and ask them to listen and list samples of the following.

COLOR	SHAPES	SOUNDS	SMELLS

Ask the students to speculate how Conrad could come up with such a lush, specific description without ever having directly experienced what he described so well. Ask them to identify some instances that they have experienced in which they imagined in great detail something that they had not directly experienced. Present the word "imaging: to visualize or make a mental image of a new experience based on similar past experiences."

THE PLANET CREON

ACTIVITY

Instructions:

1. Divide the class into groups of three. Give each group newsprint, crayons and tape. One student will draw while the other two close eyes and visualize the imaginary planet Creon. These are the conditions: "The two have just beamed down to the planet from their spaceship. The planet has no gravity, but does have oxygen and a temperate climate. Because it faces two stars, it has no night and no water."

2. The two seers are to take turns creating a picture of the planet: its inhabitants, life forms, landscape, etc. The only conditions that apply are the ones described already. The artist will sketch, as well as possible, what they describe in their 5 minute vision. After the seers are done, the artist may add any two touches he or she chooses as long as they fit the vision. Tape the finished images around the room and allow the class a few minutes to view them.

METACOGNITIVE DISCUSSION

Ask the students to describe the origins of the details in their images. How did they transform what they had experienced in the past to the new picture? What was difficult about the task? How might they use imaging in tasks that they have to do?

CLOSURE

Tell the students that one helpful place to use imaging is in goal setting. Have them record this mental menu in their LOGS.

a. **I**magine a goal (give an example from your own experience).

b. **M**entally pick a starting point (retrace your example).

c. **A**dd each step from start to finish (share yours).

d. **G**raph your steps on an imaginary map (do yours on the board).

e. **E**liminate barriers (describe some and what you did).

f. **S**ense the feeling of triumph (tell what it was like for you).

Invite each student to close his/her eyes and picture a goal (school, family, work, etc.). Talk them through each of the 6 steps of IMAGES. After you have completed all steps, do a class wraparound with a stem selection from "I learned..." "I noticed..." "I wonder..." or "I pass."

IN THE YEAR 3001

BACKGROUND When a thinker moves out of the limits of his/her own environment and explores an unknown world in the future, present day biases and restricted views are removed. In the world of fantasy, we are free to explore many possible solutions without the boundaries of the present. Problem-solving in the future gives permission for all things to be possible.

THINKING SKILL: INVENTING

FOCUS ACTIVITY Ask the students to close their eyes for a few minutes. Tell them that you are going to help them explore in their mind's eye a future world where travel is going to be far different from what it is today. (Encourage them to be very serious. It is very important that they not make any noise, comments, etc. which might disturb their neighbor's concentration.) Encourage the students to get comfortable and try to picture themselves in a space travel machine in the year 3001. What does the machine look like from the outside. See it in detail. Picture the inside. What does it look like? What are people doing? How is it propelled?

OBJECTIVE To generate ideas about future space travel.

INPUT Review Osborn's SCAMPER, and elicit examples of each micro skill.

S Substitute a part
C Combine new elements
A Adapt the object
M Modify it
     Magnify
     Minify
P Put it to new uses
E Eliminate or omit
R Rearrange parts
     Reverse the sides

ACTIVITY Instructions:

1. Divide the class into teams of 3-5. Allow ten minutes for the teams to review DOVE Guidelines. Arrange for a recorder, timekeeper, materials manager, leader and reporter (f less than 5, duplicate assignments) and plan how they will think through the task. In planning their thinking, they must review what they have learned about generating ideas.

2. Ask a few teams to review their thinking plan. The plan should outline the thinking operations important for generating ideas, criteria for success and troubleshooting hints.

3. After commenting on the plans, give this task to all teams: "Using your skills for generating ideas, you will design a space vehicle to travel in the year 3001. Your own planet is about to disintegrate and you know of no other planet within the reach of your current scientific knowledge that will sustain life. Therefore, you must depend upon your ship as a vehicle of escape as well as a possible self-contained world. You will have 20 minutes to design this ship. Describe its major internal parts, its fuel and fuel source, how it will contain indefinite life support, and how entertainment will be taken care of.

4. After the 20 minutes, you will have 10 minutes to roughly sketch the external view of the ship, as well as one or two internal views. You will use these sketches to describe all the important features of the vehicle required for survival and entertainment of the travelers.

5. Allow each team to describe its vehicle to the class.

METACOGNITIVE DISCUSSION | Ask the following lead questions:

1. Which parts of your plan for thinking did you follow?

2. Which parts did you change? Why?

3. Using the criteria you listed for the skillful generating of ideas, judge what was the best thinking you did. What can you improve?

4. What might be some ways you could apply some of the thinking skills you used in this task for generating solutions to other problems you face in your school life?

CLOSURE | "You will have 15 minutes to plan one of the following activities. You will complete the task outside of class and tomorrow you will report/present the results."

1. You must sell this space trip to possible clients. Write an ad jingle to a popular nursery rhyme tune.

2. You must sell this space trip to possible clients. Make a magazine ad (sketch, collage, etc.) which will do that.

3. Prepare a three minute news broadcast to report the coming voyage or an event on the voyage.

SHOE BOX TRANSFORMERS

BACKGROUND Brainstorming is a method of generating as many ideas about a topic as possible. Introduced to American business by Alex Osborn, brainstorming has many uses for the effective thinker. Most importantly, it teaches us to value the search for many ideas before we begin to critique and narrow our thinking to the best idea. In Osborn's approach, effective brainstorming not only *generates* ideas, it *transforms* ideas.

THINKING SKILL: TRANSFORMING

FOCUS ACTIVITY Project the 5 basic guidelines Osborn suggests as helpful conditions for effective brainstorming. Use the overhead or board to list the guidelines. Students will find it helpful to have the list in their notes for reference.

1. *No criticism.* (Accept all ideas. Hold critiquing until we have gathered many.)

2. *Free Wheel.* (Look for wild and crazy variations of all ideas. Be crazy.)

3. *Quantity is the foundation of Quality.* (We can pick the best when we have the most.)

4. *Combine.* (Add to, subtract, join ideas together in different ways.)

5. *Move Quickly.* (Don't stop to worry if an idea is ok or what you think is wanted.)

Next, ask them to think of the TV show "The Transformers." Ask several to identify why the main characters are called "Transformers" (change shapes for different jobs).

OBJECTIVE To practice transforming ideas by generating many changes.

INPUT To change and build on ideas, it helps to think in a variety of ways. Osborn suggested *9* idea transformers which help us to change or shift an idea. For instance, toy makers have taken the idea of the super hero and combined it with the idea of a robot which can do many things in different shapes: The Transformers.

Provide students with a list and discuss Osborn's *9* transformers.

1. *Adapt?* What else is like this? What other idea does this suggest? Does past offer parallel? What could I copy? Whom could I emulate?

2. *Put to other uses?* New ways to use as is? Other uses, if modified?

3. *Modify?* New twist? Change meaning, color, motion, sound, odor, form, shape? Other changes?

4. *Magnify?* What to add? More time? Greater frequency? Stronger? Higher? Longer? Thicker? Extra value? Plus ingredient? Duplicate? Multiply? Exaggerate?

5. *Minify?* What to subtract? Smaller? Condensed? Miniature? Lower? Shorter? Lighter? Omit? Streamline? Split up? Understate?

6. *Substitute?* Who else instead? What else instead? Other ingredient? Other material? Other

process? Other power? Other place? Other approach? Other tone of voice?

7. *Rearrange?* Interchange components? Other pattern? Other layout? Other sequence? Transpose cause and effect? Change pace? Change schedule?

8. *Reverse?* Transpose positive and negative? How about opposites? Turn it backward? Turn it upside down? Reverse roles? Change shoes? Turn tables? Turn other cheek?

9. *Combine?* How about a blend, an alloy, an assortment, an assembly? Combine units? Combine purposes? Combine appeals? Combine ideas?

ACTIVITY

Instructions:

1. Divide the class into groups of three. Allow each group to select an object from the many you have collected into a shoe box. (i.e. lemon, checkbook, triangle, bunsen burner, aluminum can, pencil, stapler, etc.)

2. Each group must identify to the class what the object is and how it is generally used.

3. Using Osborn's transformer list, each group will brainstorm changes they can make on the basic object so that as a TV super hero "Transformer," it could:

   a. put out a fire
   b. paint a picture
   c. kick a field goal
   d. catch a criminal in a fast escape car
   e. do three other "super jobs" selected by the group

4. With newsprint and markers you provide, the group will make three sketches of the transformed object. In each sketch it will show its new shape for one of the selected tasks.

METACOGNITIVE DISCUSSION

1. Ask each group to review its sketches and to trace how they transformed the object. Be sure they are specific about which of Osborn's Transformers they used.

2. Ask students to describe what might be some situations in which they might use the transformers to complete a task?

3. Ask students to describe what they find beneficial about thinking with the transformers? The drawbacks?

CLOSURE

In the LOG, use the *adapt* transformer to identify ways you might use idea transformers for one of the following:

1. Changing your study area
2. Improving your grades
3. Writing an essay for class
4. Improving your bedroom
5. Your choice

THE STORY GRID

BACKGROUND How items are arranged will vary on the purpose of the arrangements. A grocery store will arrange objects for shoppers' convenience: all the soups in one section, the noodles in another. A salesman will arrange his calendar by sales priorities. Stories also have a sequence or arranged pattern which is basically a combination of time and cause-effect. The characters, events, or setting may vary, but the plot will dictate the arrangement of what takes place. In all cases, a pattern emerges with "variations on a theme." The creative artist often has the most freedom and the most difficulty in composing these variations. The story grid or morphological grid is a tool that professional script writers use to change the content of stories when they have a set plot. It allows them to maintain interest and novelty without using up their creative genius.

THINKING SKILL: ARRANGING A PATTERN

FOCUS ACTIVITY Ask the students to describe their favorite cartoon serial or soap opera. If they were the story writers, what would they do to write 100 or more stories week after week? What would be some difficulties/challenges in their job?

OBJECTIVE To identify a tool for creating a variety of story sequences.

INPUT Ask students to guess about the difficulties of creating a TV show week after week with the same characters and story line.

After someone has described how hard it would be to keep interest and variety week after week with the same cast of characters, describe how Fran Stryker, writer of the Lone Ranger story, invented a method to help him keep the creativity alive with different variations in the basic story by creating the morphological or story grid.

ACTIVITY Instructions:

1. On the overhead or blackboard, show this grid.

	HERO	HEROINE	VILLAIN	CONFLICT	SETTING	THE ENDING
1						
2						
3						
4						
5						
6						
7						
8						
9						
10						

2. Ask the students to give names of anyone in history, literature, their lives, films, TV etc. whom they would call the hero. Write the first 10 in the hero column. Repeat for the heroine and the villain. (They should not try for a horizontal match up).

3. List possible conflicts (i.e. fist fight, argument, etc.) and settings (OK corral, NY City, backyard.)

4. Finally, list possible endings to a story (rode into the sunset, lived happily ever after, etc.)

5. Ask one student to provide the last six digits in his/her phone number.

6. Select one word for each column that corresponds to each number given and circle the items.

7. Assign students to groups of four. Instruct each group to take the items circled and create a story line for a TV SHOW. Allow 5-10 minutes and ask sample groups to share their stories.

METACOGNITIVE DISCUSSION
Conduct a classroom discussion by asking students the following:

1. Describe the steps you took in deciding how to make the story from the six elements. (You may want to describe how you would do it.) Encourage half of the class to listen for the differences used in deciding. Encourage the second half to listen for the similarities. Paraphrase responses to check out and extend the reports.

2. Ask for the differences that were noted. Make a list on the board. Make sure that the differences are clarified.

3. Ask for the similarities. List and clarify the responses as needed.

4. Ask the students to speculate on the reasons for the differences in thinking that went into making each story line.

CLOSURE
Ask each student to use the last 6 digits of his/her phone number and create a new story line.

OR

Ask the small groups to construct some rules for creating many story sequences even though they are limited to a set number of factors. Share the rules with the class.

OR

Ask students to share when a word grid would be helpful in (a) this class or (b) another class.

EGG-SACTLY

| **BACKGROUND** | In graduate school design classes, students often are given the challenge to use their creative skills. One school challenged students to make a robot ping pong ball scooper. Using less than $25.00 worth of materials, design teams had to create a machine to scoop up 200 ping pong balls in the shortest time. The team with the fastest time would win. This task forced students to use what they learned about identifying and solving problems. |

THINKING SKILL: DESIGNING SOLUTIONS TO PROBLEMS

| **FOCUS ACTIVITY** | Divide the class into groups of five. Give each team the following materials: (a) a newspaper (8-12 sheets); (b) 12″ of 1″ masking tape; (c) two sheets of 8 ½″ X 11″ tag board; and (d) scissors. Tell them that they are going to design a product which will protect an egg from breaking when dropped 2′ - 12′ heights. |

| **OBJECTIVE** | To design a protective package for a dropped egg. |

| **INPUT** | On the overhead or blackboard, list and explain these guidelines you *are* following: |

6 Ways To Promote Creative Design

1. Let students create the designs. Don't tell them how.

2. Break the mold. There is no one, perfect way.

3. Start from scratch. Michaelangelo's standards aren't yours.

4. Stay away from grades. No grades on this. A surprise award for the winning teams!

5. Take your time. There is a full 40 minutes for the design.

6. Think it through. There are prizes for the thinkers as well as the champs!

Tell them that there will be prizes for each of these categories: (if you have more than six groups, make up some new prizes.)

1. The Survivor. (the one egg dropped from the highest point with no cracks)

2. The Most Different Design (from everyone else's)

3. The Good Try. (Looked great, but...)

4. The Omelette. (Sorry...)

5. The Prettiest. (Enough said)

6. The Best Plan. (You know what)

7. The Most Original Cheer. (If nothing else works...)

Be sure every group wins a prize. (You are the judge.) Provide something tangible for each award.

ACTIVITY — Instructions:

1. Give each team an uncooked egg, newsprint and marker.

2. They have a three fold task.

    (a) To consider many options for their design. They must select a pattern (web, list, etc.) and record their thinking as they plan the design.

    (b) To complete the package with *only* the materials given to them. They have 40 minutes and no other limits.

    (c) To create an original cheer to be used in the "drop."

3. As soon as all groups are done or at the end of 40 minutes, prepare the drop area. Spread all newspapers out over the drop area.

4. Instruct each team to select a dropper. Each dropper will take turns dropping the design from similar heights. (3', 6', 10', 12') As an egg cracks (shows juice!) it is eliminated. Keep increasing the height until there is a champion. Clean up each mess.

5. Preceeding each drop, the teams will use the cheers to egg on the dropper.

METACOGNITIVE DISCUSSION

1. Use your chart to review your group's thinking as you explored the design possibilities.

2. What were some patterns you noticed in your team thinking?

3. What gave your team the most difficulty? How did you resolve the difficulties?

4. If you redid the design, how would you think about the task?

5. What did you learn about "designing" as a thought process?

CLOSURE — Conduct an award ceremony with each team receiving its award.

WHAT'S THE USE?

BACKGROUND Dr. Edward DeBono invented a way of thinking that he calls "Lateral Thinking." It is designed to encourage the interaction of ideas so that new and different ideas are forced to emerge. Lateral Thinking defers evaluation and forces the thinker to look at a problem in many new ways. Even the most pat solutions can be changed to create exciting possibilities. In this adaption of Lateral Thinking, students will learn to enliven solutions to standard problems by forcing new and different combinations. More importantly, it will give concrete methods for using Osborn's Brainstorming pattern...and the students just might invent a new tool or kitchen utensil.

THINKING SKILL: GENERATING IDEAS

FOCUS ACTIVITY Ask the students to recall DOVE. Ask why it is important that they use DOVE when brainstorming new ideas.

OBJECTIVE To force the generation of new ideas through Lateral Thinking.

INPUT Introduce Osborn's Brainstorming patterns to the students.

S Substitute a part

C Combine new elements

A Adapt the object

M Modify it
    Magnify it
        Minify it

P Put it to new uses

E Eliminate or omit

R Rearrange parts
    Reverse the sides

Use a chair as a thinking model. After each letter explanation, give or elicit an example of what changes they might make (i.e. **S** = substitute a part. 4 wheels for 4 legs, a glass bottom for the seat, etc.).

ACTIVITY Instructions:

1. Assign the students to partners. Each pair will have 30 minutes to develop responses to the following questions. Encourage the students to follow DOVE and defer all evaluation of their ideas until the assignment is completed.

2. Hand each pair a kitchen utensil or a work tool.

    A. Describe the object and its intended use.

    B. Brainstorm some other uses for the object. (Be creative!)

C.   If you enlarged the object 100 times, what might be some other uses for it?

D.   Change one part of the object so that you make a major change in its use.

    (1)   Your change:

    (2)   Brainstorm possible new uses.

E.   Reverse any two parts of your tool. Draw the picture.

F.   Take away one of the reversed parts and substitute a part of another tool or utensil.

    (1) Draw your new tool.

    (2) Brainstorm possible uses:

G.   Combine this tool or utensil with another into a single object. Draw it.

H.   Shrink the combined tool by 50%. Brainstorm its uses.

I.   Select one person to sell this new tool to. What advantages would you list to make the sale?

3.   Have students create a drawing of the final product on posterboard. They should select one or two of the advantages generated to make a slogan for the item. Post the items around the room and allow students to mill about and look at the items.

METACOGNITIVE DISCUSSION   Ask students the following questions:

A.   What did you learn about Lateral Thinking from the task?
B.   In your own words, how would you explain Lateral Thinking?
C.   When doing school assignments, when would be a good time to use Lateral Thinking?
D.   When else should it help to use Lateral Thinking? Explain your example.
E.   What did you find hard about Lateral Thinking?
F.   What other changes would you have made to the tool?

CLOSURE   In the LOG, have students draw a positive-negative chart. In the positive column, they should list the advantages of Lateral Thinking. In the negative column, they should list the disadvantages.

POSITIVE	NEGATIVE

THAT'S A GOOD IDEA

BACKGROUND Shooting down good ideas with "yes, buts" and "It will never fly, Wilbur" is a quick way to kill creative and critical thinking. On the other hand, major think tanks promote a positive climate in which thinkers can safely explore new possibilities without "put downs" and premature criticism.

THINKING SKILL: GENERATING IDEAS

FOCUS ACTIVITY Tell the students the story of the Wright Brothers' first plane and how they were told "It will never fly." Ask volunteers to invent a classic put down which might have been addressed to:

> Thomas Edison/Light Bulb
> Einstein/Relativity
> Michaelangelo/The Creation
> Gutenberg/The Press
> Steven Jobs/The Apple MicroComputer
> Henry Ford/The Model "T"
> Shakespeare/Hamlet

OBJECTIVE To practice ways to generate multiple ideas in a safe and secure climate for productive thinking.

INPUT Introduce the DOVE Guidelines. Indicate how important following these guidelines will be for generating an abundance of creative ideas.

> **D** = Do accept others ideas
> **O** = Originality is OK
> **V** = Variety is valued
> **E** = Energy on task is important

> Classify and discuss each of the points.

ACTIVITY Instructions:

1. Using a random number, divide the class into groups of four or five students.

2. In each group, identify the recorder, leader, materials manager, and the time-keeper. Distribute newsprint, marker, easel or wall space and masking tape to each group.

3. Assign *one* of the following means of transportation to each group: camel, flying carpet, snowmobile, fire engine, dog sled, pink elephant, hang glider, grocery cart, doll carriage, big wheel, dinosaur.

THAT'S A GOOD IDEA

4. On newsprint, the recorder will write two column headings: "improvement" and "because."

IMPROVEMENT	BECAUSE

5. The recorder will write in one improvement which will make for a more enjoyable ride (i.e. swimming pool). The person to the recorder's right will either say "I pass" or "That's a good idea because..." The recorder will write the complete statement in the "because" column. The same student will then add a new improvement or pass. No other comments are allowed.

6. Proceeding to the right, each *in turn* will indicate "a good idea, because..." This will complete several rounds until you call a halt.

7. Ask the recorder in each group to share (a) the vehicle; (b) improvements; and (c) reasons with the class. Invite all to listen to each report. Accept all responses and thank each reporter.

METACOGNITIVE DISCUSSION

1. What did you like about this activity?

2. In what ways were you helped to be more creative?

3. What do you like about your group's list?

4. What might improve your group's list?

5. Recall the DOVE Guidelines. In what other situations might they help your thinking?

CLOSURE Distribute old magazines, scissors, glue, and tack board to each group. Instruct them to use the materials to create a collage "ad" to promote sales of the new vehicle. Post the results.

DO YOU WANT TO BET?

BACKGROUND

One of the conclusions that we have reached about skillful thinkers is that they are risk-takers who use data to make sound predictions. The better they are as thoughtful students of data, the more successful they are as predictors. In essence, they do not need to take wild guesses; they take calculated risks based on a careful study. Their bets are safe bets that usually "bring home the bacon." Studies are also showing us that there is a strong correlation between the skill to make predictions in reading and the skill to make predictions in critical thinking.

THINKING SKILL: PREDICTING

FOCUS ACTIVITY

Invite one student to the front of the classroom. Show a coin and predict whether it will fall heads or tails. Have the student flip the coin and tell you whether you won or lost. Ask the class to guess how many times out of a hundred flips, it will turn up heads? out of a thousand?

OBJECTIVE

To improve the skill of predicting.

INPUT

Using the board or overhead, provide the students with this information:

A Definition of *Prediction:* anticipating what will occur with a high degree of success. (80%)
An example: X number of coin flips will turn up tails.
When it's important: in reading fiction, in scientific experiments, in detective work, in an operation, and in math problem-solving.

The menu of operations:

Base on facts.
Examine clues for probability and possibility.
Tender your bet and make a guess.

If you run into difficulty: infer from feelings, tone, attitudes and keep studying the facts.

ACTIVITY

Instructions:

1. Distribute copies of the shortened story, "The Dinner Party". Prefold the sheets on the lines.

DO YOU WANT TO BET?

THE DINNER PARTY

By Mona Gardner

The country is India. A colonial official and his wife are giving a large dinner party. They are seated with their guests - army officers and government attaches and their wives, and a visiting American naturalist - in their spacious dining room, which has a bare marble floor, open rafters, and wide glass doors opening onto a veranda.

("BET" what will happen next? Why do you think so; find data to support. Read to verify.) _____

A spirited discussion springs up between a young girl who insists that women have outgrown the jumping-on-a-chair-at-the-sight-of-a-mouse era and a colonel who says that they haven't.

"A woman's unfailing reaction in any crisis," the colonel says, "is to scream. And while a man may feel like it, he has that ounce more of nerve control than a woman has. And that last ounce is what counts."

("BET"...) _____

The American does not join in the argument but watches the other guests. As he looks, he sees a strange expression come over the face of the hostess. She is staring straight ahead, her muscles contracting slightly. With a slight gesture she summons the native boy standing behind her chair and whispers to him. The boy's eyes widen, and he quickly leaves the room.

Of the guests, none except the American notices this or sees the boy place a bowl of milk on the veranda just outside the open doors.

("BET"...) _____

The American comes to with a start. In India, milk in a bowl means only one thing - bait for a snake. He realizes there must be a cobra in the room. He looks up at the rafters - the likeliest place - but they are bare. Three corners of the room are empty, and in the fourth the servants are waiting to serve the next course. There is only one place left - under the table.

His first impulse is to jump back and warn the others, but he knows the commotion would frighten the cobra into striking. He speaks quickly, the tone of his voice so arresting that it sobers everyone.

"I want to know just what control everyone at this table has. I will count three hundred - that's five minutes - and not one of you is to move a muscle. Those who move will forfeit fifty rupees. Ready!"

("BET"...) _____

The twenty people sit like stone images while he counts. He is saying "...two hundred and eighty..." when, out of the corner of his eye, he sees the cobra emerge and make for the bowl of milk. Screams ring out as he jumps to slam the veranda doors safely shut.

"You were right, Colonel" the host exclaims. "A man has just shown us an example of perfect control."

"Just a minute," the American says, turning to his hostess. "Mrs. Wynnes, how did you know that cobra was in the room?"

A faint smile lights up the woman's face as she replies: "Because it was crawling across my foot."

2. Invite the students to silently read the first segment. When they are ready, tell them to use BET to predict what will happen next. Elicit responses by identifying the facts, discussing the clues and making solid guesses.

3. Continue through each segment.

METACOGNITIVE DISCUSSION

Invite students to answer the following:

1. Explain BET in your own words.

2. What are some times that you might use BET? (school and non-school) Explain and clarify how.

3. How is this method of reading different from what you ordinarily have done?

4. What would happen if you were to use BET in preparing for your next major test?

5. What are the strategies and disadvantages to using BET? (Make a chart.)

CLOSURE

Instruct the students to write a telegram to the President or a Congressman. In the telegram, make a prediction, based on facts you know, what will happen if a specific policy is followed.

OR

Write a telegram to the student government and make a prediction what will happen if...
Collect the telegrams and read samples.

NOTES

A NOVEL IDEA

| **BACKGROUND** | Guided Reading calls for you to lead students into predicting outcomes based on the Creative Problem-Solving Model. Predicting |

what will happen next not only heightens student motivation to read-on, but it also enhances comprehension as students are required to read with rigor, as they think critically and creatively about elements in a story.

THINKING SKILL: PREDICTING

| **FOCUS ACTIVITY** | Introduce students to "A Novel Idea" by forming groups of four students. Each group will need a discussion leader, materials manager, recorder and observer/time-keeper. |

Obtain multiple copies of several *different* age-appropriate paperback novels. Briefly, preview the themes of each novel and have groups select the one they will read in their "Book Group." (If your students are not ready for a novel, use short stories.)

| **OBJECTIVE** | To predict the outcome of a sequence of events. |

INPUT

1. Review the Creative Problem Solving Model (from Traffic Jam Strategy)

2. Define prediction and on the overhead show a web. On the first arm, mark the attributes of prediction.

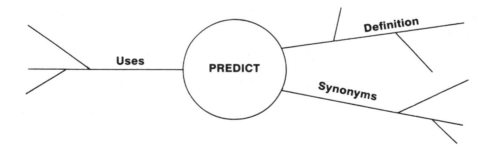

3. On a second arm, ask the class to add synonyms. On a third, brainstorm times when we use prediction.

A NOVEL IDEA

ACTIVITY | Instructions:

1. Assign students to read the first chapter. In the LOG, each will make 3 predictions about what will happen in the next chapter of their novel.

2. Vote and decide by consensus *what the group thinks will happen next* as a probable outcome of the problem situation identified. Allow ample time for groups to interact. Reinforce evidence of thinking as problem-solvers.

METACOGNITIVE DISCUSSION | Call total groups together. *Do not* try to discuss the various novels in progress. Use this time to talk about *prediction* and how the Creative Problem-Solving Model is a useful tool to develop reading sophistication. (Plus, it's just fun to try to 'outguess' the author!) Good thinkers use prediction frequently. For an excellent discussion starter, use a "whip" with this lead-in: "Predicting outcomes is similar to _____ because _____." After response-in-turn around the room, you might facilitate further discussion with some of these questions!

1. What did the authors do to build suspense? How did they help your predictions?

2. How might you adapt some of these techniques in your writing?

3. Predict what might happen if you kept a log of writer's techniques that give you clues on which to build your predictions.

At the beginning of the next period, prove the prediction through selected readings in the 'Book Groups.' Proceed from that point with a new chart each time a group meets. See if predictions improve in accuracy or if students' predictions would actually make a better story. Then lead them into the next chapter. Continue until the end. For variations in discussion after each chapter, change the stems and discussion questions. Close each discussion with a LOG entry.

CLOSURE | Have students review all LOG entries for "A Novel Idea." Instruct them to *trace* one of the following:

    a. Their predictions. What patterns did they notice?

    b. Their LOG entries. What patterns did they notice in their thinking?

    c. Their improvement in using Creative Problem Solving (CPS).

PIRATE'S MAP

BACKGROUND When reading a mystery or watching a TV thriller, many suggestions and clues are given. The reader or viewer must read between the lines, put clues together and infer what is meant. This skill of inferring is also one of the most frequently tested in reading exams.

THINKING SKILL: INFERRING

FOCUS ACTIVITY Ask students to tell you all they know about pirates. Be sure you insist on the DOVE (p. 62) Guidelines so they don't put down each others ideas. List all the answers on the board or overhead. If they have no background, assign research topics from the library about pirates.

OBJECTIVE To learn how to draw inferences from clues given.

INPUT On the overhead:

1. Define inference: The act of passing from one proposition, statement, or judgment considered as true to another whose truth is believed to follow from that of the former.

2. Provide several synonyms:
   infer, deduce, conclude, judge, gather.

3. List and explain sample times when students might use inferring as a thinking skill.

4. Give several examples from age-level stories.

   Check for student understanding by asking several to translate and explain 1-4 in their own words.

PIRATE'S MAP

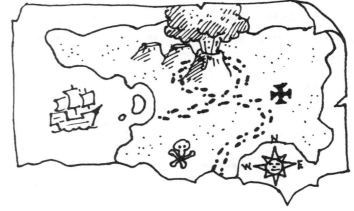

ACTIVITY

Instructions:

1. Arrange students into groups of three.
   Give each group the following clues:

   A. The partially torn map

   B. A label-free bottle
   C. A torn monopoly dollar

2. Ask one student to record. Invite each group to generate possible connections among the three objects. What do the objects tell us might have happened?

3. After five minutes, give out the second piece of paper.

4. Tell the trios to use this last clue to add to or modify their guesses on what might have occurred.

5. After the trios have the final pieces, instruct them to write a news story that includes a description of who, when, what, where, why and how it happened.

METACOGNITIVE DISCUSSION

1. Share the stories.

2. After each story, ask the following:

   A. What clues did you use in deciding what happened? Which did you ignore? Why?

   B. In arranging the clues, how accurate were the inferences? Explain.

   C. Did this trio leave out any important information?

   D. When making inferences, what would you place on a list of do's/don'ts. (List these)

CLOSURE

In your LOG, use the lists of do's and don'ts to evaluate how well you drew inferences from the clues *and* what traps you will have to avoid.

OR

In your LOG, complete the stem, "about inferences I learned..."

DIG

THINKING SKILL: INFERRING

FOCUS ACTIVITY On your desk, place a dozen items or pictures of items all of which are mechanical or electrical. Select 3 volunteers to come forward, study the materials and agree on what the objects might tell a time visitor from 1492 about our culture *if these* were the only facts.

OBJECTIVE To identify helpful ways to make sound inferences from partial data.

INPUT When we read stories, watch the news, or explore new information, we often get only partial information. From that information we have to draw conclusions or make judgments. This "filling in the missing pieces" is called inferring. It is a valued skill in our society. Most reading tests as well as the SAT test will test our ability to make inferences. A strong reader or detective will examine the given data carefully and make sound, logical judgments about how the pieces fit together.

ACTIVITY Instructions:

1. Divide the class into two teams. Each team will select a President and 5 Council Members. Each Council Member will head a work team. Every team member will have 1 team assignment.

    A. Music

    B. Art & Sculpture

    C. Business & Industry

    D. Government & Law

    E. Recreation/Travel

    F. Construction

The team headed by the Council will invent a culture. They will put into writing a description of the culture via its government (i.e. democracy, diarchy), business (i.e. money system, products), (Groups A-E), etc. Each work group will construct, find or create 3-5 objects which would represent the culture's significant beliefs, values or products as defined by the team. These must be objects, which if found in the future, would give some indication of what was most memorable or significant about the culture.

2. After each team has made its clues, it will bury the objects in an area you select no larger than 1' deep, 8' wide and 10' long. Items larger than 6" X 6" X 6" will be broken and the pieces scattered on the site. Small items may be buried whole.

3. Group F will construct a sifter from chicken wire (3' X 5'), tacks or staples and 16' of 2" X 4" wood.

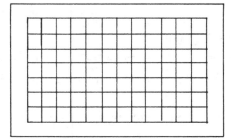

4. Teams will dig up to buried cultures, sort clues according to the A-F groups, and in each group decide what conclusions they can draw.

5. After each group of each team has drawn its conclusion, the team lead by the President will draw its whole conclusion about the found culture.

METACOGNITIVE DISCUSSION

1. Each group will present its findings.

    A. What are the significant values, beliefs and products of its society?

    B. What proof is available to back up the conclusions?

    C. How did you arrive at the conclusions? Demonstrate the thinking processes used.

    In the presentations, all members must have some active part.

2. What "rules of thinking" would be most helpful in conducting a dig? Where else might you apply these rules?

CLOSURE

Select one of these statements to complete in your LOG.

"Some discoveries valuable to my own thinking that I made on this dig were…"

"The hardest thinking in the dig came when…"

"If a space visitor found my room in a dig, he/she would conclude… about me."

HOW MANY ANSWERS?

BACKGROUND

The need for creative thinking in solving problems is clear as we reflect on a quote from Alex Osborn's book, *Applied Imagination*. "Everything in the world remains to be done or done over. The greatest picture hasn't been painted. The ideal labor contract is yet unwritten. A windproof match, an airtight bottle cap, a lifetime lead pencil have not yet been conceived. The best way to train salesmen, an easy way to keep slim, a better way to pin diapers* - all of these problems are unsolved. Not one product has ever been manufactured, distributed, advertised or sold as efficiently as it should be or someday must be..."

When we want to find solutions to a problem, it is important to follow the path of creative thinking. A critical step in the creative thinking process is the skill of brainstorming. Brainstorming generates a fluent list of possibilities.

* Published prior to "tab" diapers.

THINKING SKILL: DISCOVERING SOLUTIONS

FOCUS ACTIVITY

1. Tell students to form groups of three. Identify the person wearing the most blue to be leader. The leader will appoint the materials manager and timekeeper.

2. Review DOVE.

3. Hand out 2-3 magazines, a piece of 8 ½ X 11 poster board, glue, and scissors to each group.

4. Each group will randomly select six objects (i.e. a car, a wrench, a crane) that have little apparent likeness, (Allow 5 minutes) and cut them out.

5. Using the six objects, the group will invent a new object that has a practical use. They will cut and trim the pictures and glue together a picture of the new object.

6. They will name the object.

7. Have the groups post their inventions.

8. Discuss with the class which attributes of creative thinking they used in creating this new object. List the attributes on the board. Encourage all to contribute. After the list is complete, indicate that they will be using these same attributes in developing solutions to problems.

OBJECTIVE

To master the skills and processes helpful for developing creative solutions to problems and challenges.

HOW MANY ANSWERS?

INPUT Brainstorming is not a difficult skill, but the process can be greatly enhanced by an awareness of the elements inherent in creative thinking, by applying an identified technique systematically to the generative process and by following some basic guidelines as you facilitate the process. As a teacher of creative thinking, you can instruct students how to use this method to increase the fluency, flexibility, elaboration and originality of their ideations. To facilitate the brainstorming, a "systematic search" provides a comprehensive approach. Some concrete examples will clarify. A man wanted a bookmark that would stay in place. He happened to be an employee of 3M, the company that manufactures a wide variety of adhesive materials. His idea was to develop an adhesive for the bookmark that would stick "just enough" to mark the pages in his hymn book at church, but "unsticky" enough to allow easy removal with no damage to the page. He basically *minified* the stickiness factor of adhesive tape when he conceived the subsequently developed Post-It Note! In addition, since these "sticky fellows" have hit the market-place, an avalanche of uses have appeared, illustrating the ingenuity and fluent thinking of the consumer.

The creator of the "Big Clip" did just the opposite. He *magnified* the standard paper clip, *substituted* plastic for metal and *modified* it by using color. People in the *Overhead* episode survived through their creative ingenuity. By *putting* a safety pin *to another use,* they made a fish hook that helped them survive during their 112 day ordeal at sea in a rubber raft.

To help students generate ideas, keep in mind:

a. ***Elements of Creativity***

    (1) Fluency - quantity
    (2) Flexibility - shifts
    (3) Elaboration - detail
    (4) Originality - uniqueness

b. ***SCAMPER Techniques****

    (1) **S**ubstitute
    (2) **C**ombine
    (3) **A**dapt
    (4) **M**odify, magnify or minify
    (5) **P**ut to other uses
    (6) **E**liminate or elaborate
    (7) **R**everse, rearrange

c. ***Rules of Brainstorming - DOVE***

    (1) **D**efer Judgement
    (2) **O**pt for Off-beat
    (3) **V**ast number
    (4) **E**xpand on ideas by hitch-hiking

ACTIVITY Instructions:

1. Provide a handout to the students. Instruct each student to select one of the problem scenarios given. After a few minutes, instruct the students to find three other persons to form a group of four who have selected the same scenario.

* SCAMPER: Games For Imagination Development.

2. Identify the person who had the most hours of sleep on the previous night. That person will have the leader role. Instruct the leader to identify the recorder, the materials manager and the timekeeper/observer for the task. Have them spend a few moments reviewing the job responsibilities and DOVE before giving out the newsprint, markers and tape.

3. Each group may brainstorm questions that they wish to ask you about the scenario. After 3 - 5 minutes to identify the questions that they want to ask, instruct them to select the top three that are most important to ask. Allow each group using the first scenario to ask you one question at a time. No duplications. Once all of a group's top three have been asked by any group with the scenario, they will pass. When all the groups have used all the ranked questions, go to the second and then the third scenario. When you answer the question, be creative. They will have to live with the details that you give. For instance, about scenario one, students might ask: "Are these the only people involved." You may say "yes" or you might add some other characters. Be creative but not complicated.

THE PROBLEM SCENARIOS

A. Mary and Sue grew up together and have been close friends for more than a dozen years. For the past two years, Barry and Sue have dated regularly. Barry has taken a sudden, heavy interest in Mary and wants her to go to the Homecoming Dance with him. Mary keeps putting him off, but really wants to go to the dance.

B. Al likes his job stacking groceries at the local market. He has held the job for three years. He's using one-half of his weekly check to buy a used car. Because business has been so good, the manager has hired another stock-boy. The manager is paying the new employee, his nephew, $.20/hour more than Al.

C. Rich is a straight "A" student. He hopes to go to college for pre-med. He has two older sisters who are already in college. The family cannot afford a third full tuition and Rich is concerned that if he takes a job, his grades will suffer and hurt his chances of getting into a good pre-med school.

4. Instruct the groups to take five minutes to agree upon and record responses to each of the following:
   (a) What is the principle character's goal?   (b) What is the problem?

5. Draw a model attribute web. Have each group recorder write the problem in the center of the web. Instruct the groups to use response-in-turn without interruptions to generate possible solutions to the problem. Each person who adds an item will designate whether or not the solution is basic (main branch) or a refining or supportive solution (secondary branches). The speaker determines where the idea is placed on the web. Allow 8 - 10 minutes for this step.

   MODEL:

   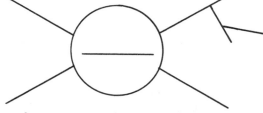

6. After the webs are done, allow five minutes for clarifying. Clarifications should be noted on the webs.

7. Instruct the recorders to make a second chart, the pro-con chart. On this chart they will record the arguments for selecting one solution to the cause of the problem. (At this point, you must decide whether you are going to give instructions for the whole process at once or step by step). As necessary, check for understanding of the instructions.

HOW MANY ANSWERS?

MODEL:

ITEM	PRO	CON
1		
2		
3		

8. Instruct each student in each group to select the one basic solution and its supporting details that he/she will argue as the one to select. This is done privately, alone, without collaboration. After selecting, each will privately list 2 - 3 reasons in support of the selection.

9. Using different color markers, each student will identify his/her favored solution and its supporting details on the worksheet. Demonstrate this.

10. In turn, each will list the item chosen and supporting (pro) arguments without duplication.

11. After all the pro arguments are listed, each will identify arguments against (con) the item that he/she put up on the pro list. (The other side of the coin!) After that is done, the person may add con arguments against any other item. If the person cannot con his/her own, that person may not con any other argument.

12. The leader will take the group through a weighted voting. Having considered carefully all arguments, each person will have three votes: a three pointer for the best solution, a two pointer for the second best, and a one pointer for the third best. The recorder will tally the votes on the newsprint. The highest vote will win.

METACOGNITIVE DISCUSSION

Ask these questions of the entire class. Remember wait-time, equal distribution of questions, cueing and encouragement. Seek multiple responses and give specific feedback about the quality of thinking used in the discussion.

1. Trace the steps used to arrive at your group's solution.

2. Which of the steps were easiest for you? Most difficult? Explain.

3. Why is it important to argue cons to your own pros?

4. When might you use a web? Give specific instances and walk us through the thinking steps you would use (i.e. topic, major ideas, details, grouping for selection, etc...).

5. What are the advantages of a web for your thinking?

CLOSURE

Construct an all class web. In the circle place one of these problems:

"Last night, your neighbor's house burned to the ground. They will have no money for 5 days (when the insurance check arrives). What can the family of six do for food & shelter?" (fire)

"You borrowed your dad's car. You ran it off the town bridge and it is now submerged in 2 feet of water in the creek. Your dad will be home in three days." (car)

"Your have a final exam on Monday. You left all your materials in your school locker. The building is locked for the weekend." (exam)

Ask the class to brainstorm solutions as you record the responses on the web.

TRENDS

| BACKGROUND | A discussion as old as the Greeks focuses on change. How does it happen? Why does it happen? Is change constant? Or are there |

BACKGROUND A discussion as old as the Greeks focuses on change. How does it happen? Why does it happen? Is change constant? Or are there some things that never change? Can we control change? One philosopher indicated that change was like a flowing river. It was always water, but always different water. Whatever position we finally take in this never ending argument, we will recognize that there is change and that it greatly affects our lives. At least to some degree, we can make descriptive statements about specific changes that are occurring around us. For instance, we can say with good evidence that our society is moving from an industrial economic base to a high tech economic base. We can say that America is becoming a more mobile society. Or we can say that electronic communications has made us a more global village with news traveling at faster and faster rates. These descriptive statements of changes which we identify in our society we call trends or markable social changes.

THINKING SKILL: GENERALIZING

FOCUS ACTIVITY Ask students to tell you some of the ways their favorite music has changed in the last three years. What is new that they like today that was not around three years ago? List these changes on the overhead or blackboard. Do the same for clothes fashions, TV and auto designs.

MUSIC	CLOTHES	TV	CARS	OTHER

OBJECTIVE To identify appropriate methods for making generalizations.

INPUT Begin by asking the students to make accurate statements about the changes that they have listed. An accurate statement will generalize or say what is true about the facts, not more and not less. They must be careful about the selection of pronouns so that the statements are limited to the facts. List and explain these qualifiers:

a. All, every, always (stated as in "Everybody does it," or implied as in "People say...") as well as none, never, nobody.

b. Most, the majority, almost.

c. Some, a few, a couple.

d. Fifteen, twenty, three or other numbers.

Remind them that the qualifiers must be accurate and provable. If not, there must be enough evidence to make the generalized statement that will hold true for all the instances of a trend that they identify.

Next, provide these definitions:

a. *a generalization:* a statement that describes what is common about all given instances. It is a rule or an all-inclusive guideline that will work in all situations when the identified conditions are present. For instance: on American streets, a red octagonal sign means "stop." A period signals the end of a declarative sentence.

b. *a trend*: a repetition of events which occurs with enough regularity that a predictable generalizable pattern is observed. For instance: in the music, clothes and car examples listed earlier in class, we can generalize about trends that are observable in what students like. We need a sufficient number of young people to buy records of a certain type such as "heavy metal" to declare a trend.

In order to make a generalization, there are four guidelines to follow. Use the acronym, RULE:

    a. Round up specific data.

    b. Uncover the patterns.

    c. Label the patterns.

    d. Evaluate the validity of the generalization with the 80 - 20 rule. (Do at least 80% of the randomly selected samples fit the pattern?)

Demonstrate RULE with the music list the students made in the Focus Activity: (a) you have the data they collected; (b) identify the patterns; (c) label the patterns; and (d) see if there are enough samples to make a generalization. Check for understanding by asking volunteers to repeat the process with cars or clothes.

TRENDS

ACTIVITY

Instructions:

1. Assign the students to groups of three. Instruct each group to select one of the following topics: vacations, car color, car size, car style, new homes, developing jobs, movies, books, TV ads, recreation, schools, home electronics, families, politics, health, food, sports.

2. In the next week, each group will scan newspapers, magazines and other available print (i.e. brochures from a car agency) for at least 25 samples or items related to its selected topic. If they are to apply the 80-20 rule so that they may make at least one accurate generalization about trends related to the topic, they will succeed in the task. For instance, if the group selects "highways" and they find a minimum of 20 pictures or articles describing the decay of the interstate system and no more than five that depict it expanding or improving, they will have sufficient data.

   If they find more than the minimum of 25, they must maintain the 80-20 ratio.

3. After they have sufficient data, they are to construct a collage with the items that support the generalization they are making.

4. If they cannot identify a trend in their topic, they may substitute some trend indicators. Indicators of possible trends must have at least 40% samples.

METACOGNITIVE DISCUSSION

Ask each group to respond to the following:

a. What is the trend that you identified?

b. Explain your evidence.

c. How strong is your evidence for the generalization you made?

Discuss with the class the following:

a. Explain in your own words the terms "Generalization" and "Trend."

b. When are some instances in which you might use the RULE Guidelines?

c. How is thinking about generalizations different from brainstorming? drawing conclusions? making analogies?

d. As you reflect on your ability to make sound generalizations, what do you do well? could you improve?

CLOSURE

In your LOG, complete one of the following:

A generalization is like...   because...

A trend is like...   because...

When I make generalizations, I need to remember...

A trend I would like to reverse is...   because...

NOTES

THE THOUGHT TREE

BACKGROUND — One thinking skill that students are challenged to use in most standardized tests is decoding analogies. From primary school basic skills tests to the Graduate Record Exam, the analogy checks student ability to acknowledge similarities and infer relationships. This emphasis is placed on the analogy because it is a strong indicator of the student's skill in understanding and communicating complex thought. During school, students will meet the analogy in a variety of forms. In addition, they will learn that the analogy is a powerful tool for expressing key ideas.

THINKING SKILL: MAKING ANALOGIES

FOCUS ACTIVITY — On the board or overhead, place this list of concrete objects: bird, carrot, tree, plane, pencil, heater, box TV, car, chalk, book, house, can, dog, boy, doll, truck, toe, bolt, ball, ice cream cone, leaf, boat, potato, box, barn, truck, cloud, sign, window, printer, cup, fish, rock, love, joy, friendliness, hope, kindness, courtesy, peace. Note that all are nouns. Illustrate the differences on this spectrum.

(Concrete _____ **Abstract)**

Ask each student to randomly select any two objects and construct this sentence: _____ is like _____ because _____.

Read some of the sentences which you will label "analogies."

OBJECTIVE — To identify several methods for making analogies.

INPUT — Begin by defining the term analogy: a comparison of two concrete objects that visualize an idea. The analogy helps us to grasp and communicate abstract ideas, to present ideas in a unique way and to identify similarities. In order to make strong analogies, follow the MAKE Guidelines:

Make a comparison of two objects (courage and rain).
Acknowledge the similarities (both can appear unexpectedly).
Keep the connection clear as you infer the relationship (courage appears out of nowhere like a summer storm does).
Express the relationship (courage, like the summer shower often surprises us with a visit).

Give students some other samples and ask them to apply MAKE as you did in the sample above (fear, cloud) (boy, puppy) (happiness, leaf).

ACTIVITY — Instructions:

1. On the overhead or board, project a thought tree. Start the class thinking about the word, love. Write it on the trunk. On the roots, brainstorm other nouns that we associate with the feeling of "love." On the branches, brainstorm words associated with spreading "love." Write these on the tree.

2. Divide the class into groups of three. Give each group a sheet of newsprint, markers, and a word taken from the focus activity list. Instruct groups to place the selected word on the trunk and then add other nouns in the roots, branches, stems and leaves.

3. Display the completed sheets and allow students to mill about for five minutes and observe the different results.

| **METACOGNITIVE DISCUSSION** | Students can create a variety of different analogies with the tree. Begin with these |

questions. Encourage multiple examples.

1. Select a noun from your tree's roots. Using the trunk word (i.e. love), create an analogy sentence (i.e. Love is like water because it flows freely.) and share it with the class.

2. Make an analogy in which you use your key word (i.e. love) and compare it to a part of the tree. (Love is like the leaves because it waves to all.)

3. In the small groups, take one of the analogies you made and use MAKE to explain your analogy. Be very specific about the thinking you did in making the analogy. (Ask several groups to share the results of this discussion.)

4. What is most important to remember about making an analogy? How can you use what you have learned about making an analogy to understand analogies that you read?

| **CLOSURE** | In the LOG, sketch a car. On the wheels, write words that you associate with wheels; on the engine, write words you associate with a motor and on the |

windows, words you connect with windows. (Wait for them to do each.) On the door, write your name. Select any three words that you have written on the car and complete this sentence three times:

"I, _____, am like the wheels of a car because _____." In the last blank use the selected word that fits. "I, _____ am like the windows because _____." "I, _____ am like the engine because _____."

NOTES

CATCH THEM
PROBLEM SOLVING

MAP A PLAN

Skillful thinkers apply their abilities to good planning. A significant skill in planning is the ability to project goals and examine what it will take to achieve the goal. This includes predicting pitfalls and obstacles and devising alternate routes.

THINKING SKILL: GOAL PLANNING

FOCUS ACTIVITY
Divide the class into pairs, give each pair a sheet of newsprint and a marker. On the board or overhead, list these situations:

1. Reaching the Moon
2. Finding the Wizard of Oz
3. Discovering Atlantis
4. Traveling to the North Pole
5. Visiting Grandmother's House

Ask students to identify the common elements in each (someone taking a trip; going someplace, having a goal based on a story, etc...). After you have discussed the items, tell each pair to select one as a basis for a planning task they will do together.

OBJECTIVE
To plan a realistic way to reach a goal.

INPUT
Identify and define each of the following words:

GOAL: a desired state or place
PITFALL: a trap
BARRIER: a block or obstacle

ACTIVITY
Instructions:

1. On the newsprint, each pair will sketch its starting point and its goal. (Model on the overhead or board).

> *The Goal
>
> *Start

2. They will sketch at least three alternate paths from the start to the goal. Each path will have at least three different pitfalls or barriers. They should sketch these in place. No words.

3. They will sketch in a picture which means they select to avoid the pitfalls and bypass the barriers.

MAP A PLAN

| METACOGNITIVE DISCUSSION | After you have joined pairs into fours, instruct the pairs to use the ABC interview |

sheet (See ABC's of Scoring Goals). Each pair will be on focus for 8 minutes (a) to describe its chart and the thinking used to make decisions; and (b) to respond to the ABC interview.

| CLOSURE | Introduce these 3 stems: |

About goal planning,

> I learned...
> I discovered...
> I wonder...

Use an all class wrap around to hear the responses.

ONE PIECE AT A TIME

BACKGROUND "All Gaul is divided into 3 parts" is a quote known to every student of Caesar's *Gallic Wars*. The military commanders knew the importance of dividing maps into smaller parts or *segments*. Today, in a high tech world, the importance of taking one piece at a time, moving step-by-step through a computer program or a strategic plan cannot be underestimated.

THINKING SKILL: SEGMENTING

FOCUS ACTIVITY Divide the class into groups of three. Give each group one of the following: an empty cereal box, a sheet of newspaper, a magazine, a box of paper clips or pencils. Instruct each trio to divide the object in three different ways. At least one way must divide the object into 3 or more equal parts; another must divide the object into 3 or more unequal parts. Allow 3 minutes before you ask the groups to share what they did. Make a master list of all the different ways to divide. Record the different synonyms used for "divide".

OBJECTIVE To understand the importance of segments in the planning process.

INPUT Using the various synonyms for the verb "to divide", create a parallel list of nouns (segments, divisions, parts, fractions) and have students explain each. After you create the list, make a second list of reasons for segmenting (i.e. to measure, to share, to plan) and a third list of uses (i.e. bridge building, road construction, getting ready for a long trip).

SYNONYMS	REASONS	USES

Explain that segmenting is an important thinking skill used in planning. On the board or overhead, sketch a road map from your town or city to the state capitol. Show how crossroads, intersections or the towns divide the trip from your home to the capitol into *segments*.

ACTIVITY Instructions:

1. Copy a state map in 8½ X 11 segments. From a full-size road map you will get about 8 segments. For a class of 32, you will need 4 copies of each segment. Select 2 sites on opposite end of the state and circle each site.

2. Give one segment to each student. They must find the 7 other segments that form the whole map. When 8 are together, in a whole map, they are to plan the trip from one marked site to the other. For the trip, they must obey the speed limit, estimate how far they can travel each hour, mark off the route and change drivers each hour and one-half. They must mark the change spots.

ONE PIECE AT A TIME

METACOGNITIVE DISCUSSION

1. Ask each group to trace its route and indicate the change spots and the number of trip segments.

2. What determined the segment size?

3. If they were given a non-travel task, such as write a paper for class, cut a lawn or study for a major test, how could they determine the segment size?

4. Where else and how would they segment a task?

CLOSURE Describe briefly, how you would plan a vacation trip. Divide the trip into segments and in your LOG explain what you have to think about in making the segments.

OR

In the LOG, create an animal analogy:

Segments are like _____ because... _____.

THE ABC'S OF SCORING GOALS

In a society where instant gratification is the norm, looking ahead, planning, taking risks, developing strategies and stretching one's self-expectations are not commonly mastered skills. It is far easier for most students to follow the TV model and constantly react to the instant impulse. Without the ability to look ahead, to set realistic goals, and to plan alternate strategies, few students will become critical thinkers who analyze situations and develop creative solutions. Goal setting is the foundation of strong problem solving. Students who learn to set achievable, believable and capable goals are students well down the road to becoming realistic and successful problem solvers.

THINKING SKILL: GOAL SETTING

FOCUS ACTIVITY Ask students to define the word "goal" as they know it, list synonyms (desires, wishes, wants, etc.) and types of goals they have (career, school, personal, etc.). Have them fill in a copy of this chart in their LOGS.

GOALS

MEANING	SYNONYMS	TYPES

OBJECTIVE To identify criteria for setting realistic goals.

INPUT Realistic problem solving begins with the A, B, C's of goal setting. A = achievable, B = believable and C = capable. These are three criteria which can help students measure the quality of their goals. Consider each.

First, *Achievable:* An achievable goal is one that the individual can trace, step by step, from his or her current place to the actual attainment. This means that the goal is clear and explicit. On the long climb to the goal, the individual knows each step in sequence, which steps are critical, and which steps may need some adjusting. For instance, Sue, an outstanding 15-year-old tennis player, wants to reach her goal, professional tennis. She has thought carefully about what she must do. She knows, for instance, that she must practice a minimum of four hours per day, continue her weight program, control her diet as prescribed by the team nutritionist, strengthen her serve, and so on. By breaking her long range goal into manageable sequenced steps, she makes her goal more achievable.

THE ABC'S OF SCORING GOALS

Second, **Believable:** A believable goal is one which is built on a careful assessment of what is within our grasp. Each of us will refine our vision of what is possible to us by our experience. Direct experience can be the best teacher; indirect experience also helps. For instance, Sue may wish to be a professional tennis player. For Sue's mother that goal was not very believable because Sue's mother neither knew, read about, saw on TV or the movies nor heard about a woman becoming a pro tennis player, the dream was virtually unbelievable. Sue and her mother both needed concrete models. For Sue's mother, there were none. Sue, however, has read about women pros in *Sports Illustrated,* saw women's tennis at Wimbledon, attended a pro tournament at Forest Hills, got an Evonne Goolagong autograph, and interviewed her next door neighbor, a pro women's coach, for the high school paper. Sue's first-hand contact with women pros made her goal believable.

Third, **Capable:** A capable goal is one built on solid assessment of one's strengths and weaknesses. The assessment is solid to the degree that one has good evidence from reliable sources of what one can and cannot do. Sue's coach is a reliable source. Weekly, she previews a videotape of Sue's practice. They keep a tally of how well Sue does with each different type of shot. They measure strength, accuracy and attention. She can compare her skills to others in her ability class as well as to women pros, to evaluate her capability.

The A, B, C's of goal setting will help students clarify their goals and bring them into a line that is more realistic. When taken together, the A, B, C's help the student form a more realistic, intertwined picture of what is desired and the best means to that goal. By learning to use the A,B, C approach, they will give themselves a tool that will set a very positive and clarifying framework for substantive problem-solving.

ACTIVITY Instructions

1. Divide students into groups of three. Assign numbers 1,2 & 3.

2. Introduce the words "clarify," "extend," "focus" and "support" by writing them on the board or overhead. Solicit several explanations and examples of each word. Instruct the students to add the words to their vocabulary lists in the notes.

THE ABC'S OF SCORING GOALS

3. The first person is the focus person. The other two in the group will focus their complete attention on the focus person for six minutes. After the focus person has had no more than three minutes to describe his/her goal with no interruptions from the others, they will ask goal clarifying questions and extending questions to draw out the focus person. In no way will they argue with the focus person. They will use good eye contact, positive body language and give non-verbal support to that person's responses. They will alternate questions for the final three minutes.

4. The focus person may select one of the following areas to share with his/her group: (handout 1)

    a. a career goal
    b. a skill goal
    c. an academic achievement goal
    d. a product goal
    e. a task goal
    f. a personal relationship goal
    g. a personal improvement goal
    h. a family goal
    i. a spiritual goal
    j. a physical achievement goal
    k. a travel goal

    The focus person will describe the goal as specifically as possible in the three minute time. One member will keep time. The focus person may wish to describe the reasons for the goal, the advantages, how it was selected, what benefits it might bring, the hardships that it presents, and so on.

5. After listening for three minutes maximum, the others in the group will alternate questions from the ABC group. (Handout 2). All questions must come from these unless it is necessary for the listeners to ask a clarifying question such as "Can you be more specific?" or Can you give us an example?". "Why?" and "Don't you think...?" questions are out of bounds.

6. Conduct a model interview. Select a goal area from your life and share it with the class. Have a timekeeper stop you after three minutes. Invite students to select questions from the list for you to answer. Don't forget the pass rule. (In fact, this is a good chance to model the OK of saying "I pass".) After three or four questions, check for understanding by asking for thumbs up, etc. On the instructions for the focus interview, clarify as needed and put the groups to work for the first round.

7. At the end of the time, instruct the focus person to give a specific "I appreciate..." to each partner for the assistance provided and to write into his/her LOG the original goal statement or any change made because of the clarification and support.

8. While the first focus person is completing the LOG entry, the others may prepare their goal statements. When you signal, the next person in the group will become the focus person. Complete this round as the first. When the second LOG entry is done, the third person will move to focus and complete the round.

THE ABC'S OF SCORING GOALS

METACOGNITIVE DISCUSSION Using a classroom wrap around, ask students in turn to respond to your processing lead-in: "From this goal clarifying activity, I learned..." Encourage all to listen carefully to the ideas. Ask volunteers to identify the similarities among ideas heard. Have a student list these on newsprint or the blackboard. When several are listed, seek multiple responses to the following questions: What conclusions can you draw from this list of similarities? Why? What general statements can you make about the worth or value of asking goal-clarifying questions? What might be some appropriate times or situations for you to ask yourself goal-clarifying questions?

CLOSURE Instruct the students to use their LOGs. They might pick a different goal from the one first discussed in their group. In the LOG, write down one appropriate question they might ask themselves in each of the three (ABC) areas for that goal.

HANDOUT 1

a. A career goal

b. A skill goal

c. An academic achievement goal

d. A product goal

e. A task goal

f. A personal relationship goal

g. A personal improvement goal

h. A family goal

i. A spiritual goal

j. A physical achievement goal

k. A travel goal

HANDOUT 2
GOAL CLARIFYING QUESTIONS

A = ACHIEVABLE

What are the steps you will have to take to accomplish this goal?
Can you sequence them?
Which are the three most critical steps? Why?
Which are the least important?
Which steps may need some adjusting? Which will cause you to adjust your own ideals, beliefs, habits or lifestyle?
How ready are you to make adjustments to reach your goal?
What will you not change or give up?
What are the major external blocks in your path?
How will you handle these?
What resources do you have which can help you? How will you use them?
What is the major hurdle? Resource?

B = BELIEVABLE

What experiences have you had which will help you achieve your goal?
Which are most critical? How will they help?
What models do you have in thinking you can reach this goal?
What tangible evidence will you have to tell you that you are successful?
What means do you have to critique your progress, give feedback and check your assumptions about yourself?

C = CAPABLE

What personal strengths do you have which will help you acheive your goal?
What are the limits within yourself that will hinder you?
How do you plan to deal with your limits? Use your strengths?
What alternatives have you considered? Are any possible?
Are you able to influence persons who can assist you? What do you intend?

AND WHAT IS YOUR PROBLEM?

"A problem well-stated is a problem half solved" wrote Charles Kettering. Indeed, many thinkers will argue that effective problem solving is most dependent on the precision and care taken in the accurate identification of the problem itself.

Problem identification is a difficult skill to master. In a society that promotes instant gratification, quick fixes and fast solutions, there is a strong attraction to grab the first solution that pops into mind. *Critical* thinkers will not fall into the quick-fix sand trap. They will step back, review the problem methodically, and distinguish a problem from its cause and from the many possible solutions. As a teacher of critical thinking, you must use your trained ear to help students see these differences in increasingly complex situations. A concrete example will clarify. You enter the kitchen, open the refrigerator and take out two hot dogs. You are hungry. Your desire is to end your hunger by eating the hot dogs. You drop your hot dogs into the frying pan and turn the flame onto low. While you are preparing the buns and mustard, the phone rings. It's your neighbor. His cat is having kittens. Forgetting your hunger, you dash across the alley and give what advice you can. An half hour later, a little more tired and a little more hungry, you return to your smoke filled kitchen. What is your problem?

Clearly, your problem is two charred sticks which will not satisfy your hunger. As you fan away and turn off the flame, you look directly at your problem, the burnt hot dogs. Ugh!

If you were to present this problem to your students, you could predict that some will misidentify the problem. Some will identify the problem as your neighbor's phone call, your carelessness in not shutting off the flame, or the kittens' birth. Others will say that the problem was insufficient thinking on your part, or the need for an automatic off switch on your stove, or more consideration by your neighbor. In the first case, the students have identified possible causes or contributing conditions for the problem; in the second, they have proposed "hidden" solutions couched in such indicators as "a need for," "a lack of," "insufficient" or "not enough of!"

THINKING SKILL: IDENTIFYING A PROBLEM

FOCUS ACTIVITY

1. Prepare the class for a random brainstorming activity by asking students to recall the DOVE guidelines. As one student recalls the meaning of each letter, have a second student explain why the guideline is important.

2. Divide the blackboard into columns and enter the headings as in the model.

GOAL GAMES	DEFENSE	OFFENSE

AND WHAT IS YOUR PROBLEM?

3. Have a student volunteer record the responses which you elicit from a succession of volunteers. First, complete the goal games column: "What are games we play(i.e. monopoly, football) which have a goal?" Second, complete the "defense" column. "How does someone stop the other teams or person from winning?" Lastly, complete the "offense" column. "How do your defeat the defense?" Encourage students to follow the DOVE guidelines, especially when divergent ideas are listed in columns 2 and 3.

OBJECTIVE To construct clear problem statements.

INPUT Poorly described problems will cause difficulty in accurate problem identification. If the problem is not accurately defined, it can't be accurately solved. The most effective way to define a problem accurately is to eliminate hidden solutions. We can often recognize hidden solutions through a number of verbal indicators.

1. "Need for..."
2. "Insufficient..."
3. "Lack of..."
4. "Not enough of..."
5. "Poor..."

When faced with problem statements that *may* be hidden solutions, there are several different checks to use.

ACTIVITY Instructions:

1. Divide students into groups of 3. Assign a role to each:

(a) *Recorder:* record information during group interaction.
(b) *Leader:* manage in-turn responses, keep answers on-task and monitor DOVE guidelines.
(c) *Materials Manager:* pick up markers, tape and newsprint; keep clean sheets taped to wall, supply new tape and markers as needed and make appropriate time checks.

2. Demonstrate on a finished newsprint model, which you have prepared, as you give task instructions.

(a) "Each group will conclude this task with lists that have 'a format' similar to this example. Make your lists readable."

> **POSSIBLE PROBLEMS**
>
> 1. Too many samples.
> 2. Not enough guidance.
> 3. Lost children.
> 4. Sunken ships.
> 5. Lost horizons.
> 6. Happy days.
> 7. Vigilant spies.
> 8. New horizons.

(b) "We are going to use formal brainstorming to construct possible *problems* that a student might face in planning a substance-free party. Here is the situation. Darlene wants to surprise her friend, Mark, with a birthday party. Because both Darlene and Mark are very active in school sports and student government, the list of friends to invite is long. If all 37 show up, even without their friends, Darlene is worried that her parents' edict against drugs and alcohol will fall apart. Last weekend, there had been a party at another friend's house and there had been heavy beer-drinking and some pot smoking. Darlene was sure she wanted a party for Mark and she wanted to obey her parents. What are the possible problems she could face?"

(c) "Your group will follow the DOVE guidelines as each person in turn lists an answer to that question. Keep going around the group until everyone in turn says 'I Pass' or the 5 minutes ends. Do not stop to explain, critique, or ask about any of the ideas. Within 5 minutes see how many problems you can list in your trio."

3. Think about the goal you are seeking to achieve. Using the burned hot dog example or other relevant incidents (Going on a date, their car stops running; while studying for an exam, the electricity goes off.), use a problem diagnosis chart.

(D) SOLUTIONS	(C) CAUSES	(B) BLOCKS	(A) THE DESIRED GOAL

(A) The *goal* is the desired result, the end product, or achievement. To analyze a real problem, clarify the goal first. (The last shall go first!) "I want to eat those hot dogs."

(B) What is *preventing* you from reaching your goal. "Ugh! My hot dogs are reduced to charcoal!"

(C) What *caused* the problem? Why are the hot dogs burnt? "I let them cook too long." "There was an emergency."

(D) What can I *do?* There are many possible *solutions.* I can go to a restaurant, or eat at my neighbors or start over with hamburgers and don't answer the phone.

4. A second option to help identify problems is to personalize a situation. What events, situations or actions frustrate, anger or disappoint you? What presses your emotional button/ "I am frustrated when X occurs" or "When Tom says or does Y, I act angry." In the 'when' clause rests the problem. Write the *when* formula on the blackboard.

When (A) <u>(Name of person or situation)</u> (B) does <u>(describe)</u>, I feel (C) <u>(describe)</u>.

        (A) + (B) = The Problem
        (C) = The Result of the Problem

AND WHAT IS YOUR PROBLEM?

METACOGNITIVE DISCUSSION

1. In your own words, explain what a problem is.

2. In your own words, explain "a hidden solution."

3. What have you learned about problem identification from this activity?

4. In stating a problem, what do you find easy? difficult?

5. In what ways can you improve your problem statements?

CLOSURE — Instruct students to complete one of the following *lead-ins* in the LOG. (Use overhead)

    (a) A problem I want to solve is...
    (b) A way I could use what I've learned today is...
    (c) About problems, I wonder...
    (d) About hidden solutions, I wonder...
    (e) In using the two step problem identification process, I feel that I...

ADVENTURES WITH THE GONDOLA BALLOON

| BACKGROUND | The giant balloons which carry passengers in the gondola have evolved over many centuries. Different uses, climates and situations |

have called for changes in its form. Some thinkers argue that the best creative problem-solving is evolutionary not revolutionary, and the gondola balloon is a good example.

PROCESS: CREATIVE PROBLEM SOLVING

| FOCUS ACTIVITY | Show students pictures of gondola balloons in flight. Discuss how they operate and speculate what value balloons would |

have in our society (i.e. meteorological research, adventure clubs, etc.).

| OBJECTIVE | To identify the components of the creative problem-solving process. |

| INPUT | Show the film "Why Man Creates." After the film is completed, show on overhead or handout the seven major points outlined in the film. Ask students to explain |

each point and to provide examples for each point from their own experience. Each student should record the points, explanations and examples in the *LOG*.

| ACTIVITY | Instructions: |

1. Divide the class into work groups of four. Provide each work group with 3 sheets of newsprint, several markers and masking tape. Instruct them to identify a leader, a time-keeper, a reporter and a recorder. Review the role-responsibilities of each.

2. Project a sketch of a gondola balloon on the screen. Tell the class that they must redesign the balloon so that (a) all members of the class can travel together, (b) travel to a climate with weather extremes from -20° to +98° F, (c) travel on a month-long flight with no stops.

3. Using what they learned from the film about creative process, each group will (a) discuss the changes, (b) agree on the changes, (c) redraw the balloon with an overall picture and 2 cut-aways for special equipment, (d) have a report of what changes they made and why they made the changes.

ADVENTURES WITH THE GONDOLA BALLOON

METACOGNITIVE DISCUSSION

1. Select several groups to explain the changes and the reasons for change.

2. Ask students to relate the changes made to the 7 points from the film. Ask them to clarify specifics of thinking they did.

CLOSURE In the LOG, invite students to reflect on (a) what they have learned and (b) how they might improve their own approach to problem-solving.

OR

In the LOG, describe how redesigning a gondola balloon is *like* the creative problem-solving process.

OR

In the LOG, write a poem about gondola balloons.

WHY MAN CREATES: Director: Saul Bass

A series of explorations, episodes and comments on creativity.

1. *The Edifice:* Believers

2. *Fooling Around:* Sometimes ideas start that way!

3. *The Process:* The work begins; discouragement.....faith.....patience.....solutions present themselves.....idea comes alive

4. *The Judgement:* Society makes its contribution to the creative process

5. *A Parable:* I am unique!

6. *A Digression:* Radical ideas threaten institutions, then become institutions which in turn reject radical ideas that become institutions!

7. *The Search:* Work in progress on new ideas; time; dead-ends; nature of the process; dilemmas; provocations

Why does man create?

- Men struggle against time, against decay, against destruction and against death
- Some have cried out in torment and in agony
- Some have fought with arrogance and fierce pride
- Some challenge the gods - matching power with power
- Some have celebrated life
- Some burned with faith
- Some have spoken in voices we no longer understand
- Some have spoken eloquently
- Some have spoken inarticulately
- Some haltingly
- Some have been almost mute.

Yet among all the variety of human expressions a thread of connection, a common mark can be seen that urges man to look into one's self and out at the world and to say:

This is what I am, I am unique, I am here, I am.

Kaiser Alum Corp.
Distributed by Pyramid Films

NOTES

INSTANT REPLAY

| **BACKGROUND** | In the past few years, sports TV has developed the instant replay to a refined science. Many professional and college coaches use |

the instant replay to review games, scout and analyze player performance. Some leagues are using the instant replay to study close referee calls. In both cases, there is the chance to review what happened and make changes. The player can learn to perform differently in the next game. A new play can be introduced. The referee's call can be changed!

THINKING SKILL: EXAMINING OPTIONS

| **FOCUS ACTIVITY** | Select a literary story or a social studies event which the students have just completed. Ask the students a series of "what if" ques- |

tions. (For instance, take the start of the American revolution: "What if the British Parliament had decided to end the taxes?" "What if the colonists had decided to live with the taxes?" "What if the Continental Congress had used the CPS Model") Solicit a variety of predictions about what would have happened as a result of the "What if's".

| **OBJECTIVE** | To examine alternative events by using the Creative Problem Solving Model. |

| **INPUT** | Review the Creative Problem Solving Model on the next page. |

| **ACTIVITY** | Instructions: |

1. Explain to the students that they are going to take the "what if" questions a step further by creating several instant replays of historic (or literary or science) events.

2. Divide the class into groups of seven. Give each group a short story, or a capsule historic event or a biographic event. Instruct the group to prepare a live enactment of the event. Everyone in the group must have an active part in the dramatization.

3. The dramatization will take the piece up to an important moment of choice. At this point it will stop and the rest of the class will brainstorm a list of possible outcomes different from what does/did happen in the event.

4. After all groups have received the list of possible outcomes, assign a random number (i.e. the last 3 digits of the tallest student's phone number). Those numbers will identify the following scenario possiblilities. The group will conduct a P.N.I. chart for each solution, analyze the chart, give its rationale and prepare the *new ending*.

5. Each group will perform the new ending.

Each group will conclude with lists that have a format similar to this:

CREATIVE PROBLEM-SOLVING MODEL

GATHER FACTS	(state "mess") Mix-up, two dates unintentional, girls are best friends - they'll know, like both , want to keep 'future' open.		
STATE PROBLEM	Keep both as friends		
GENERATE IDEAS	Stagger times; Go for it! Leave town Take both girls together Get "sub" to cover one	Forget it! Enter seminary Send gifts Write Dear Abby Confess	
ANALYZE FOR BEST 3	(1) Get Sub! (2) Go for it! (3) Confess!		

EVALUATE		POSITIVE	NEGATIVE	INTERESTING
	(1) Sub! (2) Go for it! (3) Confess	both girls might work no guilt they might decide for me	might like get caught no future	could double challenge might get sympathy votes for honesty

RATIONALE	Hope for understanding
PLAN OF ACTION	*Confess!*

METACOGNITIVE DISCUSSION

Each group will chart on newsprint how it followed the Creative Problem Solving (CPS) Model in developing the solution. After each group has presented its chart, ask these questions of the class.

1. How well did they think through the process?

2. How might they think differently about the same story and the same stop point?

3. Has the use of Creative Problem Solving (CPS) improved or hurt the story, benefited or worked against...?

CLOSURE

What are some additional "what if's" you might generate about your group's event? Record several in your LOG.

TRAFFIC JAM

In previous activities, students learned SCAMPER, BUILD, DOVE and other brainstorming skills. In addition, they have learned to analyze, classify and evaluate. When it comes time for problem solving, the students will draw on these skills to create a problem solving pattern.

Edward deBono, founder of the CORT Thinking Skills Program, tells an anecdote which illustrates the benefits of adopting 'deliberate' patterns for thinking about problems. First, he relates this situation: In a new high-rise employees are disgruntled because of the constant aggravation of having to wait for an elevator. After a group brainstorming session, one suggestion that came up for later analysis was an idea that had initially seemed way off-base, totally out of context with the problem at hand.

It had been suggested during the brainstorming that mirrors could be installed on the walls around the elevators. The reasoning was that if people were pre-occupied (looking at themselves) they wouldn't notice the wait for the elevator. Ultimately, this solution proved not only cost-effective, but client-effective, too! Creative ideation and critical evaluation *are* viable patterns for thinking in problem-solving situations!

PROCESS: CREATIVE PROBLEM SOLVING

FOCUS ACTIVITY Give the students these scenarios: "You need a ride to a track meet." "You have two dates for Friday night's show." "You ruined your brother's favorite tape." "You have TONS of homework."

Ask the students: "What do you do?" and "Without detailing exact solutions, tell the kinds of things you do when faced with similar scenarios." List the various ideas on the board which describe problem-solving approaches from students. Typically, the ideas will fall into a sequence something like this:

1. Think of choices: alternatives.

2. Rate choices; rank according to perceived outcomes.

3. Decide!

4. Take action!

TRAFFIC JAM

Tell the students: "You see, problems like these get solved all the time. Somehow, instinctively, we manage to figure our way out of messy situations. In fact, we do it so automatically, often we have never thought about how we go about doing it. Yet, we know that we think about possible choices and somehow decide on a course of action."

The human race is a resourceful lot. We are ingenious when circumstances call for ingenuity - even if we do fumble about it in our own hit or miss, random manner. We do manage to manage!

So what's the point? The point is that someone has taken the initiative to jot down this somewhat random path we all seem to follow in solving life's problems. In fact, Alex Osborn, and later, Sidney Parnes, identified key components to the Problem Solving process and outlined 'deliberate steps' to take to develop effective *patterns for thinking* in problem-solving situations.

OBJECTIVE

To use creative and critical thinking skills in a problem-solving pattern.

INPUT

By approaching a problem with the 'deliberate search' techniques of creative ideation to generate alternatives and critical analysis and to develop criteria for evaluation, the Creative Problem Solving Model illustrates the dual ways the thinking mind "searches" or scans a problem. Both divergent productive thinking and convergent-evaluative thinking comprise mindful problem-solving. On the board show the following:

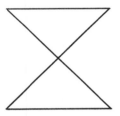

We diverge to gather all the facts, then we converge on the real problem. We engage in creative ideation to accumulate a list of alternatives, then we critically analyze those choices based on some criteria. We generate solutions and evaluate for the *best* one as we speculate on acceptance of our plan of action. Then we face the new challenges of implementation and the cycle begins again.

The experienced problem-solver is comfortable with both creative and critical patterns for thinking and knows how to use them alternately (and at times almost simultaneously) as he tackles perplexing situations.

TRAFFIC JAM

ACTIVITY Instructions:

1. To set the climate for meaningful problem-solving, begin by sharing a personal problem you've faced and the subsequent outcome. Then, place this *cloze* message on an overhead transparency:

TRAFFIC JAM

Once I had a problem twice my size. It was about _____. Believe me, it caused a terrible traffic jam in my head. I couldn't decide if I _____ or _____. Then, _____.

Probably what helped most was _____. Now, when I have a REAL HUMDINGER OF A PROBLEM, I _____. It _____.

---

2. Post 2 large sheets of newsprint on the board. List all responses generated by *cloze*.

TRAFFIC JAM	STRATEGY USED
1.	
2.	
3.	
4.	
etc.	

3. Divide students into groups of 5. On the overhead or in a handout to each group, review the Creative Problem Solving Model (see previous page). Assign a materials' manager, recorder, leader, timekeeper (20 minutes) and reporter.

4. Tell the class: "We are going to use 'deliberate' creative and critical patterns for thinking to handle a 'traffic jam.' Each manager must select a number from this set of cards." (Have numbers that correspond to the original "Traffic Jam" cloze activity. For example, if you had 30 student problems, you need cards from #1 - #30.)

5. Give the next instruction. "The number tells you which 'traffic jam' your group will tackle. On newsprint, recorder will create Column #1 of the CPS model and state the 'Traffic Jam' at the top of the sheet. Using DOVE guidelines and response-in-turn, complete your chart using the example as a reference." Check for confusion about the task.

TRAFFIC JAM

METACOGNITIVE DISCUSSION

1. In a large group format, have the reporter describe the group's chart. As the problem statement and 'final solution' or plan of action are now stated, record them on two sheets posted next to the two original "Traffic Jams" sheets. It will look like this: (Only ¼ of original list will be used!)

TRAFFIC JAM	STRATEGY USED	PROBLEM STATEMENT	OPTED SOLUTION
1. Two dates	1. Leave town	1. Keep both friends	1. Confess
2.	2.	2. not selected	2. not selected
3.	3.	3.	3.

Continue this process until all groups have reported. Allow time for interaction as enthusiastic tales unfold about finding that 'final solution'. Students will be excited about their thinking!

2. What was interesting about how you thought through the creative problem solving process?

3. How was your "deliberate" thinking similar to your usual way of getting out of a Traffic Jam?

4. How was it different?

CLOSURE

In their LOGS, instruct students to construct a + /-/? on the Creative Problem Solving (CPS) Model. If time allows, share.

	POSITIVES OF CPS	NEGATIVES OF CPS	INTERESTING QUESTIONS
1.			
2.			
3.			
4.			
5.			

PRACTICE & TRANSFER

PRACTICE

Dr. Madeline Hunter of UCLA suggests that one of the principles of effective instruction is practice. Practice, alone, however, does not make perfect. But, 'practice' can make permanent. In Dr. Hunter's articles, she elaborates on the principle of practice by addressing the issue of purpose: Is the purpose to practice *new* learning or is the purpose to *review* material for mastery? With these two distinct purposes in mind, practice is further defined:

SHORT 'MASSED' PRACTICES FOR NEW LEARNING

How much?	A small meaningful amount
How long?	Short periods of time with an intent to learn
How often?	Short periods spaced close together
How well?	Guided; monitored with specific, immediate feedback so practice is 'perfect practice.'

DISTRIBUTED PRACTICES FOR REVIEW.

How much?	Short meaningful amount
How long?	Short periods of time with an intent to learn
How often?	Spaced over time; farther and farther apart
How well?	Guided and Independent with feedback

GUIDED PRACTICE

GUIDED PRACTICE means guided practice! Teacher behaviors inherent in guiding the practice are:

1. *MOBILITY:* The teacher moves about the classroom to observe levels of understanding and ability to apply the new learning in practice exercises and correct any errors before they set.

2. *MONITORING AND ADJUSTING:* The teacher monitors student competency levels with the new learning and adjusts instruction accordingly. If there is a lot of confusion, reteaching is called for. If a few students are struggling, a small group practice session might be more appropriate.

3. *SPECIFIC, IMMEDIATE FEEDBACK:* The teacher gives specific feedback to individual students to correct mislearned skills immediately. Remember, practice does make permanent. If the student practices the skill incorrectly, it will take much longer to *re*-learn that skill. So 'perfect practice' is the purpose of guiding the practice.

4. *SHORT, REVIEW PRACTICES:* The teacher plans 'SPONGE ACTIVITIES' to better utilize transition times for needed practice and to focus students toward planned instruction.

5. *INDEPENDENT PRACTICE:* The teacher assigns short, meaningful independent practice and provides knowledge of results as soon as possible.

PRACTICE! PRACTICE! PRACTICE! Especially practice in 'patterns for thinking,' for only through frequent and repeated application of creative and critical thinking to relevant curricula, will students truly develop their skills for thinking. Only with frequent and repeated application will students become comfortable and self-initiating with 'patterns for thinking.' Remember, it takes practice to master a skill, lots of short, meaningful tries, with feedback.

If we, as educators, provide a multitude of relevant opportunities to apply the micro-skills involved in critical and creative thinking, students will begin to shift into these 'patterns for thinking' on their own! And that is the goal: to provide the necessary information and skills so kids can **THINK** both divergently and convergently as they become productive problem-solvers and responsible decision-makers. On the other hand, rigid adherence to repetitious skill and/or flooding of the classroom with ditto sheets will kill thinking.

GLOSSARY

USER'S GUIDE TO DEFINITION OF TERMS

AGREE/DISAGREE Prediction technique used to focus, diagnose and forecast.

ANALOGY A comparison showing similar relationships (i.e. apple: fruit; squash: vegetable; or a book is like a person because both relate feelings).

ANALYTIC PROBLEM-SOLVING A deliberate search that involves identifying the problem, gathering and analyzing data and justifying the best solutions.

ATTRIBUTE The distinguishing characteristic or trait.

BRAINSTORMING Group process to trigger spontaneous, fluent production of ideas.

CONCEPT MAPPING Visual diagram that illustrates relationships in free-flow of thoughts.

COOPERATIVE GROUPS Structured small groups with designated role responsibilities for each member.

CAUSE/EFFECT One factor (or set of factors) determining the outcome; chain of events.

'CLOZE' A structure similar to a 'fill-in-the-blank' format that permits divergent answers.

CLUSTERING Free-flowing technique to plot spontaneous verbal associations used in writing to initiate, focus or elaborate.

CREATIVE THINKING Using skills of application and synthesis to generate ideas; producing new ideas.

CREATIVE PROBLEM SOLVING A somewhat hierarchical model to generate alternatives and evaluate choices. The process includes fact-finding, problem-finding, idea-finding, solution-finding and acceptance-finding.

CRITICAL THINKING Using skills of analysis and evaluation to determine the worth of ideas; critiquing.

DEDUCTIVE REASONING Reasoning from a general rule to a specific case; i.e. does it fit the rule or generalization?

DECISION-MAKING Judging choices and basing final selection on evaluation of criteria.

EXPLICIT SKILL Teaching a thinking skill as the content of the lesson (i.e. teaching classification as a skill of organization).

FISHBONE A diagram used in analytic problem solving to show relationship.

FLOW CHART Sequential diagram to show possibilities or choices.

FORCED RESPONSES Strategies to structure responses from all students such as whip, wrap arounds, signals and systematic sampling.

GUIDED IMAGERY Imagination exercise directed orally by a leader.

HEX MESSAGE Cluster of hex shapes used to structure writing.

HUMAN GRAPH Simulation of a graph with participants selecting a position along a continuum to indicate choices in a hypothetical decision.

INDUCTIVE REASONING Reasoning from specific examples to a general rule; i.e. given the facts, what generalization can be made?

JIG-SAW MODEL "Pieces" of a project are assigned to small groups, then synthesized into a complete picture.

MACRO-SKILLS Critical and creative processes comprised of several micro-skills, i.e. given the facts, what generalization can be made?

METACOGNITIVE PROCESSING Thinking about thinking; tracking how one thinks, using structured discussion or written records.

METAPHOR MODEL Elaboration of a metaphor by using more than one part in the comparison (i.e. an argument is like a fire; the insult is the spark; the reaction is the kindling, etc.).

MICRO-SKILL The skill taught in isolation (i.e. classification, sequencing, compare, contrast.)

P.N.Q. Evaluating the Positive, Negative, Questionable aspects of an issue.

PATTERNS An identifiable flow of how one approaches thinking.

PROBLEM-SOLVING Specific strategies that use creative synthesis and critical analysis to generate viable alternatives to perplexing situations.

RANKING A rating system that forces prioritization of choices.

REINFORCERS Verbal and non-verbal teacher behaviors that positively support developing student behaviors.

TARGET ANALYSIS A visual to help identify priorities.

THINKING LOG A student log of visual or verbal entries reflecting personal reactions to learning.

TRANSFER Bridging the micro-skills (i.e. classification) into content areas in the classrooms and in real-life situations; application.

VENN DIAGRAM Overlapping circles used to compare and contrast.

WAIT-TIME A strategy to promote thinking that uses 3 - 10 seconds of silence following a teacher-initiated question or a student response.

WHIP Response-in-turn around the room; may pass. (Same as Wrap Around)

WORD TREES Stream of consciousness, word by association diagram used to generate creative thinking.

WRAP AROUND Response-in-turn; may pass. (Same as Whip)

BIBLIOGRAPHY

REFERENCES

Academic Preparation for College. The College Board (1983). New York, New York.

Ainsworth-Land, Vaune and Fletcher, Norma. *Making Waves With Creative Problem-Solving.* D.O.K. Publishers, Inc., New York, New York, 1979.

Alexander, Cynthia and Cowell, Juliette. *Mapping Insights.* Learning Insights, 1983.

American Federation of Teachers. *50-State Survey on Critical Thinking Initiatives.* Washington, D.C.: American Federation of Teachers, 1985.

Anderson, L.W., and B.F. Jones. "Designing Instructional Strategies Which Facilitate Learning for Mastery." *Educational Psychologist 16* (1981): 121-138.

Anderson, R.C., and P.D. Pearson. "A Schema-Thoretic View of Basic Processes in Reading Comprehension." In *Handbook of Reading Research,* edited by P.D. Pearson. New York: Longman, 1985.

Anderson, T.H. "Study Strategies and Adjunct Aids." In *Theoretical Issues in Reading Comprehension,* edited by R.J. Spiro, B.C. Bruce, and W.F. Brewer. Hillsdale, N.J.: Erlbaum, 1980

Anderson, T.H., and B.B. Armbruster. "Content Area Textbooks." In *Learning to Read in American Schools: Basal Readers and Content Texts,* edited by R.C. Anderson, J. Osborn, and R.J. Tierney. Hillsdale, N.J.: Erlbaum, 1984.

Armbruster, B.B., L.H. Echols, and A.L. Brown. *The Role of Metacognition in Reading to Learn: A Developmental Perspective* (Volta Review 84 [1982]: 46-56). Urbana, Ill.: University of Illinois Center for the Study of Reading, 1983.

Bellanca, James. *Quality Circles for Educators.* Illinois Renewal Institute Inc., Illinois, 1984.

Bellanca, James. "Quality Circles in Education." *The Principal's Principles.* Chicago. 1984.

Bellanca, James. *Skills For Critical Thinking.* Illinois Renewal Institute, Inc., 1984.

Bellanca, James; Fogarty, Robin; and Opeka, Kay. *Patterns For Thinking,* Illinois Renewal Institute, Inc., 2d. Edition. 1985.

Bellanca, James and Fogarty, Robin. *Teach Them Thinking: Mental Menus,* IRI Group, 1986.

Bellanca, James. *Planning For Thinking.* Illinois Renewal Institute, Inc., 1986.

Berliner, D.C. "The Half-Full Glass: A Review of Research in Teaching." In *Using What We Know About Teaching,* edited by P.L. Hosford. Alexandria, Va.: Association for Supervision and Curriculum Development, 1984.

Beyer, Barry. "Common Sense About Teaching Thinking Skills," *EDUCATIONAL LEADERSHIP.* November 1984, pp. 57-62.

Beyer, Barry. "Improving Thinking Skills-Defining the Problem," *PHI DELTA KAPPAN.* March 1984, pp. 486-490.

Biondi, A. (ed.) *The Creative Process.* Creative Education Foundation, Inc., D.O.K. Publishers, Inc., 1972.

Black, Howard & Sandra. *Figural Analogies.* Midwest Publications, CA 93950.

Bloom, Benjamin. *All Our Children Learning. A Primer for Parents, Teachers, and Educators.* McGraw-Hill Book Company, London, 1981.

Bloom, Benjamin S. (Ed.) *Taxonomy of Educational Objectives: Cognitive Domain.* New York, David McKay Company, Inc., 1956.

Brown, A.L. "Metacognitive Development and Reading." In *Theoretical Issues in Reading Comprehension,* edited by R.J. Spiro, B.C. Bruce, and W. F. Brewer. Hillsdale, N.J.: Erlbaum, 1980.

Burns, Marilyn. *The Book of Think or How To Solve a Problem Twice Your Size.* Little, Brown & Company, Boston, 1976.

Campbell, T.C., Fuller, R.G., Thornton, M.C., Peter, J.L., Petterson, M.Q., Carpenter, E.T., & Narveson, R.D. (1980). A Teacher's guide to the learning cycle. A Piagetian-based approach to college instruction. In R.G. Fuller, et al. (Eds.), *Piagetian Programs in Higher Education.* Lincoln, NE: ADAPT, University of Nebraska-Lincoln, 27-46.

Carnine, D., and J. Silbert. *Direct Instruction Reading.* Columbus, Ohio: Charles E. Merrill, 1979.

Carpenter, E.T. (1980). Piagetian Interviews of college students. R.G. Fuller, et al. (Eds.), *Piagetian Programs in Higher Education.* Lincoln, NE: ADAPT, University of Nebraska-Lincoln, 1980, pp. 15-21.

Carpenter, T.P., Corbitt, M.K., Kepner, H., Lindquist, M.M., & Reys, R.W. (1980). Problem solving in mathematics: National Assessment Results. *Educational Leadership, 37,* 562-563.

Chase, Lawrence. *The Other Side of The Report Card.* Scott Foresman, Inc., Glenview, IL, 1975.

Clark, Barbara. *Growing Up Gifted.* Charles E. Merrill, 1983.

Clement, J. (1982a). Algebra word problem solutions: Thought processes underlying a common misconception. *Journal for Research in Mathematics Education, 13,* 16-30.

Clement, J. (1982b). Students' preconceptions in introductory mechanics. *American Journal of Physics, 50,* 66-71.

Commission on Reading of the National Academy of Education. *Becoming a Nation of Readers.* Springfield, Ill.: Phillips Bros., 1985.

Convigtona, M.V., Crutchfield, R.S., Davies, L., & Olton, R.M. (1974). *The Productive Thinking Program: A Course In Learning To Think.* Columbus, OH: Merill.

Costa, Arthur. (ed.) *Developing Minds,* Alexandria, VA: ASCD, 1985.

Costa, Arthur L. "Mediating the Metacognitive," *EDUCATIONAL LEADERSHIP.* November 1984, pp. 57-62.

Costa, Arthur L. "Teaching For Intelligent Behavior," *EDUCATIONAL LEADERSHIP.* October

1981, pp. 29-32

Craik, F.I.M. and R.S. Lockhart. "Levels of Processing: Framework for Memory Research." *Journal of Verbal Learning and Verbal Behavior II* (1972): 671-684.

DeBoer, Anita L. *The Art of Consulting,* Arcturus Books, Chicago, IL. 1986.

Duchastel, P.C. "Textual Display Techniques." In *Principles for Structuring, Designing, and Displaying Text,* edited by D. Jonnasen. Englewood Cliffs, N.J.: Educational Technology Publications, 1982.

Durkin, D. "What Classroom Observations Reveal About Reading Comprehension Instruction." *Reading Research Quarterly* 15 (1978-79): 481-533.

Easterling , J. & Pasanen, J. (1979). *Confront, Construct, Complete.* Rochell Park N.J., Hayden Publishing Company.

Eberle, Bob and Stanish, Bob. *CPS For Kids.* D.O.K., Buffalo, NY, 1980.

Eberle, Robert F. *SCAMPER Games For Imagination Development.* D.O.K. Publishers, Inc., NY, 1971.

Eberle, Bob. *Visual Thinking.* D.O.K. Publishers, Buffalo, NY, 1982.

Edwards, Betty. *Drawing on The Right Side of The Brain.* J.P. Tarcher, Inc., Los Angeles, 1979.

Eggen, Kauchak, Harder. *Strategies for Teachers.* Prentice-Hall. 1979.

Elbow, Peter. *Writing Without Teachers.* Oxford University Press, NY, 1973.

Ellison, C. "Science Preparation of Students, Teachers is Debated." *Education Week,* 1 May, 1985, p.26.

Ferguson, Marilyn. *The Aquarian Conspiracy.* J.P. Tarcher, Inc., NY, 1980.

Feuerstein, R., and M.R. Jensen. "Instrumental Enrichment: Theoretical Basis, Goals, and Instruments." *The Education Forum* (1980): 401-423.

Fiestrizer, C.E. *The Making of a Teacher.* Washington, D.C.: National Center for Education Information, 1984.

Fiske, E. "Concern Over Schools Spurs Extensive Efforts at Reform." *New York Times,* 9 September, 1984, pp. 1, 30.

Gallagher, James J. *Teaching The Gifted Child.* Allyn & Bacon, 1975.

Gallelli, Gene. *Activity Mindset Guide.* D.O.K. Publishers, Inc., NY, 1977.

Gardner, et al. National Commission on Excellence in Education (1983). *A Nation at Risk: The Imperative for Educational Reform.* Washington, DC: Department of Education.

Gifford, B.R. "We Must Interrupt the Cycle of Minority-Group Failure." *Education Week,* 20 March, 1985, Sec. IV, pp. 24-17.

Glatthorn, Alan. *Differentiated Supervision.* ASCD, Alexandria. 1984

Good, T.L., and J.E. Brophy. *Looking in Classrooms.* Cambridge, Mass., Harper & Row, 1984.

Good, Thomas. "Teacher Expectations & Student Perceptions." *EDUCATIONAL LEADERSHIP.* February, 1981.

Gordon, W.J.J., and Tony Pose. *Activities in Metaphor.* Porpoise Books, Cambridge, Massachusetts.

Gordon, W.J.J., and Tony Pose. *Teaching is Listening.* Porpoise Books, Cambridge, Massachusetts.

Gordon, Wm. J. *Synectics: The Development of Creative Capacity.* 1968 pap.1.25 (00825, Collier) Macmillan.

Guilford, J.P. *Way Beyond The I.Q.* Creative Education Foundation, Buffalo, NY, 1975.

Hansen, J., and P.D. Pearson. "An Instructional Study: Improving the Inferential Comprehension of Good and Poor Fourth-Grade Readers," *Journal of Educational Psychology.* 75 (1983): 821-829.

Harnadek, Anita. *Basic Thinking Skills, Analogies-D.* Midwest Publications Company, Inc., 1977.

Harnadek, Anita. *Critical Thinking,* Midwest Publications, P.O. Box 448, Pacific Grove, CA 93950.

Harnadek, Anita. *Basic Thinking Skills, Patterns.* Midwest Publications, Inc., CA, 1977.

Herber, H.L. *Reading in the Content Areas (Text for Teachers).* Englewood Cliffs, N.J.: Prentice-Hall, 1978.

Hodgkinson, H.L. *All One System: Demography of Schools, Kindergarten Through Graduate School.* Washington, D.C.: Institute for Educational Leadership, 1985.

Howey, K., W. A. Matthes, and N.L. Zimpher. "Issues and Problems in Professional Development." Commissioned paper prepared for the North Central Regional Educational Laboratory, Elmhurst, IL, September, 1985.

Jenkins, J. "Remember the Old Theory of Memory? Well, Forget It!" *American Psychologist* 29 (1974): 785-795.

Johnson, Roger & Johnson, David. *Learning Together & Alone.* Prentice Hall, Inc., NJ, 1975.

Johnson, Roger & Johnson, David. *Circles of Learning.* ASCD, Alexandria, 1984.

Jones, B.F., M.R. Amiran, and M. Katims. "Teaching Cognitive Strategies and Text Structures Within Language Arts Programs." In *Thinking and Learning Skills: Relating Basic Research to Instructional Practices* Vol. 1, edited by J. Segal, S.F. Chipman, and R. Glaser. Hillsdale, N.J.: Erlbaum, 1985.

Jones, B.F., and W.G. Spady. "Enhanced Mastery Learning and Quality of Instruction." In *Improving Student Achievement Through Mastery Learning Programs,* edited by D.U. Levine. San Francisco: Jossey-Bass, 1985.

Karplus, R. (1974). ***Science Curriculum Improvement Study Teachers Handbook,*** Berkeley, CA: University of California, Berkeley.

Larkin, J. "Research on Science Education." In ***Computers in Education: Realizing the Potential,*** edited by A. M. Lesgold and F. Reif. Washington, D.C.: Office of the Assistant Secretary for Educational Research and Improvement, 1983.

Larkin, J. H., McDermott, J., Simon, D. P., & Simon, H. A. (1980). Expert and novice performance in solving physics problems. ***Science, 208,*** 1335-1342.

Maraviglia, Christie. ***Creative Problem-Solving Think Book.*** D.O.K. Publications, Inc., 1978.

Maria, K., and W. H. McGinitie. "Reading Comprehension Disabilities, Knowledge Structures, and Non-Accommodating Text Processing Strategies." ***Annals of Dyslexia*** 32 (1982): 33-59.

Markle, S. M. "They Teach Concepts, Don't They?" ***Educational Researcher*** 4 (1975): 3-9.

Mayer, R. E. "Aids to Text Comprehension." ***Educational Psychologist*** 19 (1984): 30-42.

McCloskey, M., Carmazza, A., & Green, B. (1980). Curvilinear motion in the absence of external forces: Naive beliefs about the motion of objects. ***Science. 210.*** 1130-1141.

National Commission on Excellence in Education. ***The Nation Responds.*** Washington, D.C.: Secretary of Education, U.S. Department of Education, 1984.

National Consortium for Educational Excellence. ***An Agenda for Educational Renewal: A Report to the Secretary of Education, United States Department of Education.*** Nashville, Tenn.: Vanderbilt University, Peabody College, 1984.

National Institute of Education. ***Who's Keeping Score?*** Washington, D.C.; McLeod Corporation, 1980.

Nickerson, R. S. (1982). ***Understanding Understanding,*** (BBN Report No. 5087).

Nickerson, R. S. (1983). Computer programming as a vehicle for teaching thinking skills. ***Journal of Philosophy for Children, 4*** (3 & 4).

Nickerson, R. S., Perkins, D. N., & Smith, E. E. (1984). ***Teaching Thinking,*** (BBN Report No. 5575).

Nickerson, R. S., Salter, W., Shepard, & Herrnstein, J. (1984). ***The Teaching of Learning Strategies,*** (BBN Report 5578).

Nisbett, R., & Ross, L. (1980). ***Human Inference: Strategies and Shortcomings of Social Judgment.*** Englewood Cliffs, N.J.: Prentice Hall.

Noller, R., Parnes, S., & Biondi, A. ***Creative Action Book.*** New York: Scribner's, 1976.

Noller, R., Treffinger, D., and Houseman, E. ***It's A Gas To Be Gifted*** or ***CPS For The Gifted and Talented.*** D.O.K. Publishers, Inc., Buffalo, NY, 1979.

Noller, Ruth. ***Scratching The Surface of Creative Problem-Solving:*** A Bird's Eye View of CPS. D.O.K. Publishers, Inc., Buffalo, NY, 1977.

Osborn, Alex F. ***Applied Imagination.*** Charles Scribner & Sons, 1979.

Palinscar, A. S., and A. L. Brown. "Reciprocal Teaching: Activities to Promote Reading With Your Mind." In *Reading, Thinking, and Concept Development: Strategies for the Classroom,* edited by T. L. Harris and E. Cooper. New York: The College Board, 1985.

Parnes, Sidney. *Aha! Insights Into Creative Behavior.* D.O.K. Publishers, Inc., Buffalo, NY, 1975.

Parnes, Sidney. *Creativity: Unlocking Human Potential.* D.O.K. Publishers, Inc., Buffalo, NY, 1972.

Pearson, Craig. "Can You Keep Quiet for Three Minutes," *Learning,* Palo Alto, February, 1980.

Pearson, P. D., and M. Leys. "Teaching Comprehension." In *Reading, Thinking, and Concept Development: Strategies for the Classroom.* edited by T. L. Harris and E. Cooper. New York: The College Board, 1985.

Peters, T. and Austin, N. *Passion for Excellence.* Random House, Inc., NY, 1985.

Peters, T. and Waterman, R., Jr. *In Search of Excellence.* Warner Communication Company, NY, 1982.

Polette, Nancy. *Exploring Books for Gifted Programs.* Scarecrow Press, 1981.

Problem Cards: Attribute Games and Problems. Webster Division: McGraw-Hill Book Company, NY 1966. (ESS Science Series).

Raths, Louis. *Teaching for Thinking.* Merrill, 1967.

Resnick, L. B. "Cognitive Science as Educational Research: Why We Need it Now." in *Improving Education: Perspectives on Educational Research.* Pittsburgh, Pa.: University of Pittsburgh, Learning Research and Development Center, 1984.

Rico, Gabriele L. *Writing the Natural Way.* J. P. Tarcher, Inc., Boston, 1983.

Rohwer, W. D., Jr. "Prime Time for Education: Early Childhood or Adolescence?" *Harvard Educational Review* 41 (1971): 316-341.

Rosenshine, B. "Teaching Functions in Instructional Programs." *Elementary School Journal* 83 (1983): 335-351.

Rosenshine, B., A. Harnischfeger, and H. Wallberg. *Classroom Programs for School Improvement.* An advisory paper for the North Central Regional Educational Laboratory, Elmhurst, IL: March, 1985.

Rowe, Mary Budd. "Science, Silence and Sanctions," *Science & Children.* 6: 11-13, 1969.

Rumelhart, D. E. "Schemata: The Building Blocks of Cognition." In *Theoretical Issues in Reading Comprehension,* edited by R. J. Spiro, B. C. Bruce, and W. F. Brewer. Hillsdale, N.J.: Erlbaum, 1980.

Scardamalia, M., Bereiter, C., & Fillion, B. (1979). *The Little Red Writing Book: A Source Book of Consequential Writing Activities.* Ontario, Canada: Pedagogy of Writing Project, O.I.S.E.

Schallert, D. L. "The Role of Illustrations in Reading Comprehension. In *Theoretical Issues in Reading Comprehension,* edited by R. J. Spiro, B. C. Bruce, and W. F. Brewer. Hillsdale, N.J.: Erlbaum, 1980.

Schoenfeld, A. H. (1980). Teaching problem-solving skills. *American Mathematical Monthly, 87* (10), 794-805.

Shuell, T. J. "The Concept of Learning in Modern-Day Cognitive Psychology." Paper presented at the annual meeting of the Northeastern Educational Research Association, Ellenville, New York, October, 1984.

Shulman, L. S. "Understanding Pedagogy: Research for the Improvement of Teaching and Teacher Education." In *Improving Education: Perspectives on Educational Research,* Pittsburgh, Pa.: University of Pittsburgh, Learning Research and Development Center, 1984.

Sirkin, J. R. "'All-Black' Education Agenda Advocated; Press for Excellence Seen at Odds With Equity Goal." *Education Week,* 8 May, 1985, Sec. IV, pp. 1, 27.

Snyder, D. P. *The Strategic Context of Education in America* (Future-Research Tech. Rep.). Washington, D.C.: National Education Association, Professional and Organization Development/ Office of Planning, 1985.

Southern Regional Education Board. *Teacher Preparation: The Anatomy of a College Degree.* Atlanta: The Southern Regional Education Board, 1985.

Spiro, R. "Constructive Processes in Prose Comprehension and Recall." In *Theoretical Issues in Reading Comprehension,* edited by R. J. Spiro, B. C. Bruce, and W. F. Brewer. Hillsdale, N.J.: Erlbaum, 1980.

Sternberg, Robert J. "Intelligence as Thinking and Learning Skills," *EDUCATIONAL LEADERSHIP.* October, 1981, pp. 18-20.

Task Force on Education for Economic Growth. *Action for Excellence: A Comprehensive Plan to Improve Our Nation's Schools.* Washington, D.C.: Education Commission of the United States, 1983.

Tolkein, J. R. R. *The Hobbit.* Ballantine Books, NY, 1937.

Torrance, E. Paul. *The Search for Satari and Creativity.* Creative Education Foundation, Buffalo, NY; and Creative Synergetics Associates, Great Neck, NY, 1979.

Trowbridge, D. E., & McDermott, L. C. (1980). Investigation of student understanding of the concept of velocity in one dimension. *American Journal of Physics, 48* (12), 1010-1028.

Tversky, A., Kahneman, D. (1974). Judgment under uncertainty: Heuristics and biases. *Science, 185,* 1124-1131.

Underwood, V. L. (1982). Self-management skills for college students: A program in how to learn. Unpublished doctoral dissertation, University of Texas.

von Oech, Roger. *A Whack on the Side of the Head.* New York. Warner Books, Inc., 1983.

Wallace, Robert and Editors of Time-Life Books. *The World of Leonardo. 1452-1519.* Time Incorporated, NY, 1966. (Time Life Library of Art).

Warner, Sylvia Ashton. *Teacher.* Vintage Books, NY, 1972.

Wason, P. C. (1974). The psychology of deceptive problems. *New Scientist, 63*, 382-385.

Weber, Patricia. *Promote...Discovering Ways to Learn and Research.* D.O.K. Publishers, Inc., Buffalo, NY, 1978.

Weber, Patricia. *Question Quest: Discovering Ways to Ask Worthwhile Questions.* D.O.K. Publishers, Inc., Buffalo, NY, 1978.

Weinstein, C. E., and R. E. Mayer. "The Teaching of Learning Strategies." In *Handbook of Research on Teaching* (3d ed.), edited by M. C. Wittrock. New York: Macmillan, in press.

Weinstein, C. E., Underwood, V. L. (1983). Learning strategies: the *how* of learning. In J. Segal, S. Chipman, & R. Glaser (Eds.) *Relating Instruction to Basic Research.* Hillsdale, N.J.: Lawrence Erlbaum Associates.

Whimbey, Arthur. *Intelligence Can Be Taught.* Innovative Science, Inc., NY, 1975.

Wiant, A. A. *Transferable Skills: The Employer's Viewpoint* (Information Series No. 126). Columbus, Ohio: The Ohio State University, National Center for Research in Vocational Education, 1977.

Williams, Frank E. *Classroom Ideas for Encouraging Thinking and Feeling.* D.O.K. Publishers, 1970.

Winograd, P. N., and V. C. Hare. "Direct Instruction of Reading Comprehension Strategies: The Nature of Teacher Explanation." In *Learning and Study Strategies Research: Issues in Assessment, Instruction, and Evaluation,* edited by E. Goetz, P. Alexander, and C. E. Weinstein, New York: Academic Press, in press.

Wittrock, M. C. "Applications for Cognitive Psychology to Education and Training." In *Cognitive and Affective Learning Strategies,* edited by H. F. O'Neil, Jr. and C. D. Spielberger. New York: Academic Press, 1979.

Additional resources to increase your teaching expertise...